Walking in community with Leighann, we know firsthand that she has lived the things she teaches. What you are reading is a work that has been tested. Leighann is a living testimony that radical pursuit of a relationship with Jesus through prayer will result in a radically changed life. Jump in . . . draw close . . . and be changed . . . by a faithful life of prayer.

—TRAVIS COTTRELL

WORSHIP LEADER, BETH MOORE CONFERENCES/RECORDING ARTIST

The quoted ideas expressed in this book (but not Scripture verses) are not, in all cases, exact quotations, as some have been edited for clarity and brevity. In all cases, the author has attempted to maintain the speaker's original intent. In some cases, quoted material for this book was obtained from secondary sources, primarily print media. While every effort was made to ensure the accuracy of these sources, the accuracy cannot be guaranteed. For additions, deletions, corrections, or clarifications in future editions of this text, please write Freeman-Smith.

Unless otherwise noted all Scripture quotations are taken from:

The Holy Bible, New International Version (NIV) Copyright © 1973, 1978, 1984, by International Bible Society. Used by permission of Zondervan Publishing House. All rights reserved.

Scripture quotations are taken from:

The Holy Bible, King James Version (KJV)

The Holy Bible, New King James Version (NKJV) Copyright © 1982 by Thomas Nelson, Inc. Used by permission.

The New American Standard Bible®, (NASB) Copyright © 1960, 1962, 1963, 1968, 1971, 1972, 1973, 1975, 1977, 1995 by The Lockman Foundation. Used by permission.

The Holman Christian Standard Bible™ (HCSB) Copyright © 1999, 2000, 2001 by Holman Bible Publishers. Used by permission.

Cover Design by Kim Russell / Wahoo Designs
Page Layout by Bart Dawson

ISBN 978-1-60587-372-5
ISBN 978-1-60587-410-4 (Special Edition)

1 2 3 4 5—SBI—16 15 14 13 12

Printed in the United States of America

Oh God, Please Help Me with my Doubt

LEIGHANN MCCOY

Table of Contents

Introduction

Surely the arm of the Lord is not too short to save, nor his ear too dull to hear.

— ISAIAH 59:1

I love looking for just the right verse to write in the introduction to my *Oh God, Please* books. Which, of the hundreds of promises found in Scripture, do I want to challenge my reader with in *this* book?

Here it is: Isaiah 59:1.

Think about Isaiah's words. What was he thinking the moment he scripted them on animal skin? Were people in his day disconcerted over unanswered prayer? Were they baffled by the silence of God? Did they wonder whether He was even "up there"? Or, maybe they credited God as Creator but left Him at that—some lofty ethereal being that put all of creation in place then chose to sit idly by and watch from a distance (certainly not a personal being eager to be engaged in the daily grind of life).

What prompted Isaiah to pen these words (or quill them)? Maybe men and women surrounded him who lived life on their own terms and expected God to do what they told Him to when they told Him to do it. I don't know. I do know, however, that Isaiah was quick to point out in the fifty-ninth chapter of his book that *if* his readers were having a problem with God's answers to their prayers, the fault was neither with God's ability ("Surely the arm of the Lord is not too short to save") nor His availability ("nor his ear too dull to hear").

I want to pick up right here with Isaiah, this great prophet of old. I suppose you are reading the introduction to this book because you have questions about prayer that need answers. I hope that, like me, Isaiah's words challenge (and maybe even frustrate) you. If so, I want you to hold tight to Isaiah 59:1 as you read this book and let God show you why many of your prayers seem to linger for quite a long time without any answers.

And as your prayers linger, know this: your unanswered prayers do not remain so because God is unable to give you answers. His arm is long enough to save. And your unanswered prayers do not remain so because God refuses to listen to you. His ear is sharp enough to hear. God is able and He is listening.

Still, there are reasons that your prayers remain unanswered. As you learn those reasons, I hope that you grow in your confidence that God is eager to answer your prayers. What kind of God would He be if He didn't answer prayer? In fact, God does some of His greatest work in these seasons of our lives—seasons of doubt and frustration; seasons that are created by God's seeming silence, resistance, and reluctance.

Oh God, Please is a series of books that will help you discover your powerful privilege of prayer. As you read these books, you will confront the voices that barge their way into your mind and war against you when you pray. You will learn how to take your thoughts captive to the lordship of Christ (2 Corinthians 10:5) and channel your heart cries into canals that draw you closer and closer to the heart of God and the mind of Christ.

When you read these books, you will learn that prayer is a relationship—not a list, not a meeting or a method. Every time you pray the demons shudder, and the devil will do whatever he can to convince you that your prayers are powerless. It's this argument that Isaiah was refuting when he told the

Israelites that God's arm could reach into their lives and His ear could hear their heart cries.

Each book in the *Oh God, Please* series will remind you that your all-powerful, all-loving God longs to demonstrate His power and love in and through your life as you partner with Him in His kingdom work. You partner with God when you pray. God is more interested in teaching you to pray than you are in learning. He is also more interested in answering your prayers than you are in making your requests known.

Welcome to *Oh God, Please Help Me with My Doubt*. The book you're holding in your hands will help you capture and subdue the voice of doubt, whose goal is to eat away at your faith until nothing is left but bitterness and disillusionment. In the first section of this book, you will learn to recognize God's voice. You will develop the ability to hear Him when He responds to your prayers. Then you will learn what to do when God doesn't respond, when you are faced with His silence. While wrestling with the silence of God, you will discover five keys you can use to delete doubt from your prayer life. Then you will visit with the Israelites as they camped on the outskirts of the Promised Land and see what occurred when God's people applied or did not apply these keys to their lives. Then before this book comes to an end you will examine several doubts one at a time. Together we will define, dissect, and then defeat each one. My prayer is that by the time you complete this book you will have experienced God's removal of most, if not all, of the doubts that infect your prayers.

PART 1

God Speaks

At no point in history was God ever silent. God has always communicated with his people in some way or another. We can rest assured that if God wants something said, it will be heard. It thus behooves us not to determine whether God speaks today, but how He does it.[1]

—

DENVER CHEDDIE

CHAPTER 1

Does God Talk?

My God, my God, why have you forsaken me? Why are you so far from saving me, so far from the words of my groaning?

— PSALM 22:1–2

I f you are reading a book that addresses doubt (related to prayer), then most likely you are suffering the silence of God. You're not alone. If we'd all be honest, every one of us has suffered God's silence. We're in good company.

David wrote the verse printed above. These are the exact same words that Jesus cried out on the cross. Later in the same prayer David also wrote, "Do not be far from me, for trouble is near and there is no one to help" (Psalm 22:11).

Know this: God's silence is not a result of your doubt. Sometimes He is silent. In those times it is quite OK to cry out and beg Him to speak. A bit later we are going to carefully examine another of David's prayers where he did just that. But in the first few chapters of this book, we are going to discuss the language of God. Perhaps you've never really "heard" God's voice, and you wonder whether He speaks at all.

A Conversation

I'll never forget the night my daughter Kaleigh, six years old at the time, put me through the inquisition: "Mommy, if God speaks to you when you pray, what does He say? How do you hear Him? I pray, and I ask Him to talk to me, but He never does. He never says a thing!"

After I recovered from the good shock of seeing my very young daughter struggling with a very big spiritual concept, I then tried to give her my good church answer: "Well, Kaleigh, honey—here's how it works. I talk to God, and then I wait to hear from Him. I hear from Him mostly when I read the Bible. Some people call the Bible 'God's Word.'"

"So, He doesn't really talk to you?"

"No, not the way you and I are talking to one another right now. When God talks, He talks to my heart."

Well, that didn't make sense at all to my six-year-old, and she couldn't leave it alone: "Mommy, why did God make our ears if He didn't mean to use them when He talks to us?"

I tried to pull all my vacation Bible school memories out of storage in my head and could not, for the life of me, remember ever having heard any-one even try to answer that. So, I decided I was certainly not going to be the first one and responded, "Kaleigh, I don't know."

> Jesus also assured His listeners that those who belong to God will hear God too.

Wouldn't it be great if every time we bowed to pray God just opened the windows of heaven, sent Jesus crawling through, and let Him sit with us in bodily form for just a while?! Of all the pray-ers (people who prayed) whose experiences are recorded in God's Word, the only one who got to speak to God face to face was Moses.[2] Scripture doesn't tell us that Jesus had this kind of audience with God. But, just like David, Jesus did say that He heard God's "voice" (see John 8:26). Jesus also assured His listeners that those who belong to God will hear God too (see John 8:47).

Oh God, Please . . .

This is a great book to read with a group of friends. Questions at the end of each chapter can guide your discussion. In a journal record your thoughts and your answers to these questions. Jot your prayers. By the time you finish reading *Oh God, Please Help Me with My Doubt*, you will have a solid record of the way God answered your prayer. Here are some questions to ponder and discuss with others.

1. How would you describe God's voice?

2. How does God speak to you?

3. How can you be sure the voice you are hearing is God's?

For those who do not know Him, He might seem like a silent God. I couldn't tell Kaleigh when she was six, but she and I both believe that we hear God's voice today. While our God does not normally speak with a voice that our human ears can hear, He is definitely not silent.

Pray: *Oh God, I feel like the psalmist when he cried out for assurance that you were listening to his prayer. I call out to you but don't sense your presence. I long to hear your voice. Jesus said that I would hear; please, Lord, speak to me in a way that I can understand.*

CHAPTER 2

God Speaks through His Word

Your word is a lamp to my feet and a light for my path.

— PSALM 119:105

J ust as I told Kaleigh, most often God speaks to me through His Word. The other day my heart was struggling with a situation that seems desperate. By desperate, I mean that the plans being considered now—the ones that are set in motion—seem to be moving some people I love in the opposite direction of God's best for their lives. I was talking to God about my fears, and I was sharing with Him the hurt my heart feels when I try to imagine what all might be about to transpire. (We'll talk more about this later, but for now I'll say that anytime we use the words *imagine* or *imagination* in our vocabulary in relationship to fear, anxiety, or dread, we need to be sure to reel those *vain imaginations* in.)

Before I share more of the particular instance of God speaking to me, first let me tell you this: your Bible wants you to write in it! Bible verses are made to be highlighted and underlined; your Bible is made to be jotted in and marked in many other ways. I would not have heard God's voice so clearly last week had the passage of Scripture that God used not been underlined. On the day that I was struggling, I was leafing through the pages of my Bible looking for a verse to use during the message I deliver on Wednesday nights at church. In the middle of my search, I found a passage of Scripture that was written specifically for me—not for Wednesday night's message but in response to Tuesday morning's prayer.

Several years ago, during another crisis, God had showed Kaleigh a passage of Scripture in Jeremiah that seemed to be God's word to me, so she shared it with me. How do I know? In the margin beside the underlined verses, I had written, "Kaleigh pointed me here on [date]." Here I was almost two years later flipping through the pages of Jeremiah, and the verses I'd underlined then were unbelievably specific to the cry of my heart that I lifted that morning. God spoke to me through His Word.

A Love Story

In order for God to speak to you through His Word, you must read it. You've got to read God's Word on a daily basis. His Word speaks best when you read it consistently. God's Word speaks best the more familiar you are with it. I encourage you to read God's Word from beginning to end. Read all of it. Sure there are parts that are not as inspirational as others, but as you grow more familiar with the Word of God, you will learn His language. It is a language of love, and it is woven throughout all of Scripture. (Don't be afraid to use tools to help you make sense of the Bible. Commentaries, Bible studies, books—all of these are great resources to help you understand God's Word. Just be careful not to let the tools take the place of the Book itself.)

> God's Word speaks best the more familiar you are with it.

When you are struggling to hear God's voice, camp out in the Psalms. I'm especially fond of Psalm 143. We're going to discuss this psalm in detail later, but for now, know that the Psalms are full of reassurance that you are not alone if you are crying out and you sense that God is not giving you His full attention. You can transform many great Psalms into prayers of your own. I do this often in my quiet time. I take the psalmist's prayer and make it my own. Here's what I did with David's Psalm 23 just a few weeks ago:

> *You are my shepherd—I will never be lacking. This IS fact. Any lack you sense is there because Satan wants you to live in the shadow of doubt—doubting God's provision for you.*
>
> *A good shepherd puts you in the best places. Sometimes you'd rather be somewhere else. But He is keeping you here.*
>
> *Oh God, thank You for restoring my soul! I have no fear of evil because You are with me. Your rod and staff (tools of discipline) they comfort me. I rest because I know that You will keep my Enemy away and You will keep me from going astray.*
>
> *Right in front of my Enemy You invite me to a feast where I am provided for—and blessed. And You pour Your love over me. Thank You, Lord. Thank You for Your goodness and Your mercy.*

God speaks through His Word. This is the primary way that He communicates with us.

Oh God, Please . . .

Discussion Questions

1. When is the last time that God spoke to you through His Word? Which Scripture did He use? How did those verses apply to your life?

2. Just for fun, read Psalm 54 and make it into a prayer.

3. Share three verses from the Bible that speak most often to you. My three are: Jeremiah 29:11, Isaiah 40:28–31, and Philippians 4:19.

Pray: Read God's Word, but before you read, say this prayer: *Lord, I believe Your Word is true. Speak to me through it today. I want to hear from You. I will respond to whatever You tell me today with a solid "yes" and "amen"* [this translated means, "so be it."].

CHAPTER 3

God Speaks through Other People

But encourage one another daily, as long as it is called Today, so that none of you may be hardened by sin's deceitfulness.

— HEBREWS 3:13

During the days when the Old Testament was being written, God often spoke through other people. Unbeknownst to them, as they shared the message God gave them to speak, they were writing those messages to us. We call those men (and women) prophets (and prophetesses). Many might believe that God no longer speaks through prophets, and perhaps He doesn't use this method of communication as much as He used to because we have the written Word of God. Still, He speaks through other people today.

Here's how He does this.

God puts a Bible verse or a thought into the mind of one of His followers during his or her quiet time. Immediately that person knows the message is for another. So, in obedience to the sense of urgency that person gets from God, they share what was received. It might be through a phone call, e-mail, or in person.

Someone did this to me today. I received an e-mail with a two-sentence message and a Scripture reference. When I receive messages like this, I either know that they are in direct response to one of my a prayers or questions, and I immediately know how to apply what they are telling me. If I'm not sure how their message relates to what I'm going through, I "put it on the back burner" (this is what one of my messengers tells me to do with his messages) and wait for what might be coming into my life in the near future. Most often I eventually understand what God has said to me through that other person.

Face to Face

Another way God speaks through other people is during conversation. I have several very good friends who I like to call my "kindred spirits." They "get" me. They're the ones who I let my guard down with, the ones I can truly be myself with. They don't judge me harshly because I'm a pastor's wife, and they don't necessarily hold me to a higher standard because I write books and speak at retreats (although they'd be justified to do so because God holds teachers to a higher standard). When I am going through a period of confusion, these are the friends who I share with.

In turn, they share with me what they've learned from their own walks with God. We talk about Scripture and share how God's kept His promises in our lives. One of these friends in particular is my faith-builder-upper. My husband Tom can always tell when I've spent time with Karen. She has a way of refreshing and reviving my spirit. I believe again when I talk with Karen.

I want to be a faith-builder-upper for others. Don't you? I want to be a woman who other women can trust—one who is safe and one who has such a dynamic walk with God that just the time I've spent with Him encourages others.

Not only do we hear God's message to us through others, but God also delivers messages through us. When you communicate God's messages to others, be sure to qualify what you have to say with this, "While God might use me to communicate to you, know that I am an imperfect vessel. Be sure to verify what I'm saying with Scripture and talk to God about it yourself." You need to do the same when others speak to you.

Sometimes we are in such a difficult place that our pain penetrates the hearts of good people, and they, in their attempt to encourage us, might share with us "a message from God" that didn't come from God. I had one friend who was terribly shaken by this experience. She was infertile for years, and she suffered through her infertility much like I did—with lots of wailing, gnashing of teeth, and arguing with God. Finally, after giving quite a public testimony at our church, she discovered she was pregnant. But several months into her pregnancy, she was told that her baby had a serious issue. The prognosis was not good. Without a miracle he would most likely be born prematurely and die soon after. She and her husband (along with her family, friends, and church) prayed that God would perform that miracle. I argued with God that she was in the perfect posture to really shout out His glory! We believed, trusted, claimed Scripture, and basically did everything we could to walk with her through her trial.

> Not only do we hear God's message to us through others, but God also delivers messages through us.

But one well-meaning, generous-hearted saint did more than that. He took her aside one night after church and gave her "a word." He assured her that her baby would indeed live and that God had great plans for that child's life. She clung to his words like a lifeline. It kept her hoping and trusting and walking in faith through every doctor's visit and all the test results. But when her baby died forty-five minutes after his premature birth, she was devastated. And the highest hurdle to jump was the "word" this well-meaning prayer warrior had given her.

When she came to me asking what she was to do with that man's "word," I told her that she had to understand that he was merely dust and that his heart was certainly right while his interpretation of what he'd heard from God was unfortunately (obviously) wrong. I explained that most likely his heart got in the way of God's real word. After all, what would she have thought had he told her that her baby would die? I assured her that God did have a plan for her baby's short life and that He certainly had a plan for hers, but that she'd have to find her answers in God. I encouraged her to take hold of God for herself and not let go—and to always put other people's "words" secondary to her own understanding of what God was saying to her.

God does speak through other people, but that method of communication needs to be secondary to God's message that comes directly to you through the reading of His *Word*.

Oh God, Please . . .

Discussion Questions

1. Have you ever received an encouraging "word" from someone? What was it, and how did it strengthen your faith?

2. Have you ever delivered a "word" to another person? How did you know it was from God? How did that person receive it?

3. Do you know someone who consistently builds your faith? What is that person like? How do you feel when you spend time with him or her?

Pray: *Father, thank You for giving us the "one anothers" in our lives who encourage us and build us up. Help me to recognize Your voice when You choose to deliver a message to me through another believer. Use me as a voice of encouragement and as a speaker of truth to others as well. Oh God, speak to me, for I am eager to hear Your voice.*

CHAPTER 4

God Speaks through Dreams and Visions

"In the last days," God says, "I will pour out my Spirit on all people. Your sons and daughters will prophesy, your young men will see visions, your old men will dream dreams."

— ACTS 2:17

Take a minute to read Matthew 1:20–21 and imagine what might have happened to Mary and Jesus had God not sent an angel to speak to Joseph through a dream.

A Gift

I've had one God-sent dream and one vision—a dream occurring when asleep and a vision occurring when awake. I know that these were from God because He used them to speak directly to me.

My dream came when I was in the eighth grade. My Sunday school teacher, who happened to be one of my father's best friends, had died in a car accident. His son was my age, and my teacher's untimely death was hard to comprehend. While I was still processing the grief of his fatal accident, I spent a week with my grandmother. During this time my cousin's two-year-old son choked to death on a hotdog. Such a terrible tragedy!

Not once but twice two people died unexpectedly and way before their time. These deaths troubled me, especially when I accompanied my grandparents to the little boy's "wake" and actually saw that precious redheaded toddler lying so still on the satin pillow. Even as a thirteen-year-old, I wrestled with God. I struggled when I prayed because I couldn't make sense of these deaths.

In my dream I was lying in bed when my mother brought me a card. Although I didn't have any pain, I knew the card was for me and that it was a "get well" card. As I opened the envelope and took the card out, I saw a picture of a river surrounded on either side by thick, lush forest. (This particular dream was in color. I've heard that we don't always dream in color so we notice when we do.) Suddenly the picture on the card came to life, and I was actually standing on the shore of that river when a beautiful white staircase (I'm assuming it was made of marble) came down from the sky. With a quick little jump, I began climbing those stairs, and my heart started racing with anticipation and joy. (The only thing I can liken it to is the anticipation I felt as a child on Christmas Eve when I couldn't wait for morning to come.) The higher I climbed, the more excited I became. At the top of the stairs I could see three robed figures. Somehow I knew they represented God— maybe the Father, Son, and Holy Ghost. When their identity registered with me, I realized that I was dying.

I put the pieces of my dream together. I had been laying in my bed sick. My mother brought me a "get well" card, and I was not going to be well. I was well in heaven, however, and felt more alive and healthier than I'd ever felt before. The dream spoke directly to my spirit more than to my senses, and mostly the sense of my own death was accompanied by fullness of peace, joy, and excitement.

Once I realized this was death, my death, I thought I was no longer dreaming, but that the dream was my reality and I was actually leaving this earth to go live in heaven. I couldn't wait! My heart wanted to rush ahead, but my head made me stop halfway up the staircase. I looked up where I couldn't wait to be embraced by the figures standing there, but then I looked back where I realized my mom would be so sad that I'd gone. I didn't wrestle with leaving this life behind; I wrestled with her being sad. Reluctantly I turned back and descended the stairs.

Before I got to the bottom, I was back in my bed. I opened the card my mother had given me and saw that it was addressed to Mr. Bridges, my Sunday school teacher. It was then that I woke up for real. I looked around my room and realized the whole thing had been a dream—me being sick, my mom giving me the card, and especially my journey up and then back down the stairs. As I lay in my bed wide awake, I also realized that the picture I saw on the card was the exact one that surrounded the baptistery in my church's little chapel. I knew it was all a dream, but I also knew that this was no ordinary dream. It was a dream gift—a gift given to me by my loving Father to help my teenaged head and heart come to a better understanding of what happens to believers (and babies) beyond our last earthly breath. I was so excited about what I had experienced that I couldn't wait to share it with my family the next morning at breakfast.

They might have thought I was crazy, but I knew God had spoken to me in a dream. And because He used that dream to give me a glimpse of what it might be like to pass from this life into the next, I was quite all right with that. God used the dream to settle my heart toward death, and that sense of peace that I had in the eighth grade revisited me a few years ago when I was diagnosed with cancer. It revisits me every time we bury someone "before their time."

God also speaks through dreams that He gives other people. A few weeks ago a woman called me on my cell phone. I hadn't heard from her in years. She'd served as our secretary at the church, but she'd been gone a long time and we'd lost touch with each other. She wanted to visit me and tell me about several bizarre dreams she'd had. It was quite strange, she said, and she didn't really know what it meant, but God had given her an urgency that Tom and I were under spiritual attack and that she needed to share her dreams. She said that God assured her that I would know what they meant.

Well, to tell you the truth, I thought it was all a bit odd. I'm not what you'd call a charismatic Christian, and I tend to raise my eyebrows at things like dreams and visions even though I have had one of each. But, I trusted my old friend and she piqued my curiosity so I agreed to meet her. I actually called one of my prayer partners and asked her to pray for me. Diane

> God used the dream to settle my heart.

had told me the dreams were disturbing, and I certainly didn't want the devil to use her words to cause me anxiety and stress.

I'm not going to share her dreams with you. They were indeed strange, but the strangest part of it was that I did know exactly what God was saying to me through Diane's dreams. They verified the spiritual attack Tom and I already knew we were under, and they delivered a direct warning to me so that I was more aware of the powerful role I have in my own battle to protect my marriage and my home. I appreciated Diane's obedience to come and share her dreams with me. She took a great risk in doing so. I was also humbled that God chose to speak to me through her dreams.

Oh God, Please . . .

Now before you dismiss me as a dreams-and-visions kind of gal, let me remind you that other than one of each in my own life and just a few in the lives of my friends, I do not bank my entire experience with God on dreams and visions. That would be dangerous. In fact, when God gave me a vision, I was so taken aback by it that I begged Him to verify His message in His Word. I simply said, "Lord, if this vision is from You, show me what it means in Your Word." And, He did. In fact, the first five words in the passage of Scripture God sent me to were these: "What I am saying is."[3]

Discussion Questions

1. Have you ever had a personal experience with a dream or a vision? If so, share your experience and the message God delivered to you through it.

2. Does it make you nervous to consider this method of communication from God? Why or why not?

3. Can you recall any dreams or visions recorded in Scripture? How did those who received them treat this method of communication from God?

4. Do you think that God speaks in dreams and visions today? Why or why not?

Pray: *Lord, I am open to any method of communication that You want to use to speak to me. I am so eager to hear Your voice, to connect my heart to Yours, that I will receive even dreams and visions. I will also verify what I experience on the solid truth of Your Word. Speak, Lord; Your servant is listening.*

CHAPTER 5

God Speaks through Worship

But thou art holy, O thou that inhabitest the praises of Israel.

— PSALM 22:3 KJV

The Bible speaks consistently of the power of praise. Joshua led the Israelites in a praise march around Jericho, and with the blast of trumpets Jericho's city walls crumbled and the Israelite army tasted the first victory in the Promised Land (Joshua 6). Many years later when Jehoshaphat, king of Judah, was faced with a vast army that was too much for him, he led the people of Judah to seek help from the Lord. Once they had prayed and fasted and heard from God (through the prophet Jahaziel, son of Zechariah), Jehoshaphat assembled his troops for battle. You might think that he'd place his best marksmen or maybe even his most courageous and seasoned warriors in the front. But he didn't. Jehoshaphat "appointed men to sing to the Lord and to praise him for the splendor of his holiness as they went out at the head of the army, saying: 'Give thanks to the Lord, for his love endures forever'" (2 Chronicles 20:21).

As the choir sang, the Lord worked. I wonder what would have happened had the men refused to praise God *before* He rescued them. The praise came first and then God engaged His power. Second Chronicles 20:22–26 tells the rest of the story. "As they began to sing" God set ambushes against the armies that were assembled together to create the enormous enemy force. The men in the vast army rose up against one another. They fought and slaughtered one another. By the time the

Israelite army arrived at the battlefield, everyone was dead. All Jehoshaphat and his men had to do was carry off the plunder. They appropriately named the battlefield the Valley of Beracah, which means Valley of Praise.

The Lord Inhabits the Praises of His People

When you and I assemble to worship, we posture ourselves for God to show up. When God comes into the gathering of the saints, He communicates His presence to them. I've witnessed this presence of God in various worship settings. Once I was in a great cathedral in London when a boys choir was singing. Few others were in the vast hall, but the sun was streaming through the stained glass and hundreds of years of praises were echoing in the sound of those boys' voices—I sensed the presence of a holy God in that place.

> The praise came first and then God engaged His power

Another time I waited in line for two hours to get into a church service in Brownsville, Florida, just outside Pensacola. An Assemblies of God church had been "experiencing revival" for many months, and word of the revival reached Thompson's Station, Tennessee. Tom and I wanted to see what was happening. I don't mind confessing that I was skeptical about the "manifestation" of God's presence in that place. I was way out of this Baptist girl's comfort zone.

As I waited in line for the doors to open, I voiced my reservations to the pastor and his wife who were standing in line with us. They were AG pastors from somewhere in the U.S., and they were quite excited to be on the threshold of "experiencing" God in that church. Here's how our conversation went, "So, what is so powerful about this place? What is God going to do here that He's not doing anywhere else? Why here? And what does it matter what we experience in there even if it is sensational?"

The pastor smiled knowingly and simply said, "If God is doing a real work here in Brownsville, it will not matter so much what happens to you *in* this place as it does what happens through you when you return home." I liked his answer.

The church service was beautiful and very much in order. People were participating freely in worship (much more freely than I'm accustomed to but not without order). At the end of the service I was not much changed (at least I didn't feel like I was), but I did sense the presence of God. However, when Tom and I returned home God moved in powerful ways in the life of our church. Over the next two years He solidified Tom as a pastor, restored peace to our conflicted little congregation, and brought more than one hundred new members to us. Ever since then we've not had a year go by that God hasn't sent more than one hundred new people our way. Tom and I attended the revival in the summer of 1997.

Hardly a Sunday goes by at Thompson's Station Church when someone doesn't weep during worship. Why the tears? Because God inhabits the praises of His people. If they come in need of comfort, God's Spirit gives comfort. If they come with unconfessed sin, God's Spirit delivers conviction. If they come desperate, God's Spirit offers hope.

The Ministry of Worship

I received an e-mail from a woman who had been a desperate guest one Easter Sunday. I'd offended her at a speaking engagement. I know that's not what you expected to read, but I did.

I was chatting freely over lunch when I went into a passionate explanation of why God hates divorce. I didn't say anything that was not true, but I had no business talking so freely when I had only limited knowledge of my audience. Unfortunately this woman was going through a divorce at the time, and she was especially sensitive to the quick judgment and pat answers the church seemed to offer in her darkness. I, of course, didn't know this.

But instead of writing me off, she and I struck up an e-mail relationship, and I was able to minister comfort and compassion to her. She told me that she wanted to worship with us on Easter morning. While I was glad that she wanted to visit, I knew that we had a drama planned, and of all things, that drama would portray a broken marriage. I gave her the heads-up, but she wanted to come anyway. I met her outside our worship area, and we sat together during the service. I noticed that she wept the entire time. I felt miserable and wondered why God allowed this woman, who was already hurting, to be in a place where we seemed to be rubbing salt in her wounds. When she left for home, I hugged her and told her how much God loved her, and assured her that I would be praying for her.

> God inhabits the praises of His people.

I figured I'd never hear from her again, but the next week I received a lengthy e-mail from her. She told me that when she'd left her home that past weekend, she'd put things in order and her head and heart were set on killing herself. I gasped—I had no idea her desperation went so deep. She went on to say that she wanted to visit our church on Easter, that being the last thing on her agenda. She told me that from the moment she walked into the building she sensed the presence of God. She described His presence as heavy and strong. She said that when we sang she could almost hear Him speak audibly the words of the songs, and that during the dramatic presentation He covered her with His peace. She told me that by the time she left her heart felt a new sense of hope, and she knew that no matter what she was returning home to her Lord and Savior would be with her and He would see her through.

Tears streamed down my cheeks as I read her e-mail. God speaks through worship—even when we can't see how He does! If you are suffering the silence of God and you are not gathering with the saints for worship, on a regular basis, then go to church! Go to a church where worship is real, and experience the powerful presence of God.

I am sorry that I have to do this, but I need to add a word of warning to you. Not all churches experience the presence of God in worship. Many of them are simply going through the motions. This was happening in "church" when Jesus came to earth. Don't go to those churches unless God's called you there to partner with Him in bringing them life. Go to a church that is growing. Attend a church that is making a difference in the world today. You will know which churches are experiencing the presence of God in genuine worship by examining their fruit. If they are actively engaged in missions, in ministry, in prayer, and in Bible study, and if they are growing numerically and in spiritual maturity, God's presence is among them. Life is too short not to be where the action is. Henry Blackaby made this phrase quite popular in his book *Experiencing God:* look to see where God is working and join him.

Oh God, Please . . .

Discussion Questions

1. Have you ever been in a worship gathering where you were certain God was there? What was it like?

2. Have you experienced God's comfort in worship? His conviction? Has your hope been renewed? Share with someone what this was like.

Pray: *Father, thank You for inviting me to come into Your presence through worship. Thank You for creating me with a heart like Yours, one that responds to music. Give the worship leaders at my church Your wisdom in leading our congregation in worship. Lead me in worship; help me to shut my eyes to the people around me and instead focus on You and You alone. Help me to worship You in spirit and in truth without being concerned about what others might think of me when I lift my arms or bow my knees, or if a tear streams down my cheek. I love You, Lord, and I want to honor You when I worship.*

CHAPTER 6

God Speaks Directly to Your Heart

I am the good shepherd; I know my sheep and my sheep know me.
— JOHN 10:14

God speaks directly to our hearts through impressions, understandings, revelations, and assurances. This is the reality I could not explain to my six-year-old. It's actually difficult to explain to you here. The only thing I can liken this method of communication to is the way in which I "speak" with my twelve-month-old granddaughter.

Misty doesn't truly communicate with words. She knows a few words—Nana happens to be one of them—but she hasn't put them together yet. I'm not sure whether she knows I'm Nana or whether she thinks our little dog is Nana. However, she does communicate with me. If I haven't seen her for a little while, my daughter brings her to me and Misty immediately tenses every muscle in her body, lights up with a smile, and grunts with delight while she shakes her tiny fists. You might find her behavior strange, but to me she's saying, "Nana, I'm so glad to see you! I love you and I've missed you!"

At other times she holds me with both arms, lays her head on my shoulder, and lets her breath out in a deep sigh. You may think that's sweet, but to me she's saying, "Nana, I love you and I am satisfied with you." When she spends the night with me, I sometimes peek in on her in the mornings and watch her play without her knowing it. On the good mornings, she chatters when she plays. The minute she catches me watching her,

her eyes get big, she smiles at me, then she makes a sweet baby sound that says, "Good morning, Nana! I'm ready to get up!"

Misty communicates with me. While I've described her body motions, I hope I've also conveyed the sense of love, peace, security, and joy that she gives me—and that I give her—simply by the two of us being together. In fact, this very moment she's helping me type as she rests in my arms. She's telling me, "Nana, I'm tired. I need to go to bed, but good luck getting me there."

From Heaven to Heart

God communicates directly to my heart in much the same way this precious baby does. (Did I mention that I am smitten with her?) When I sit quietly reading the Bible, I can sometimes feel His strong arms wrap around me. If I get really still, I can sense His presence right there with me. I have this funny way of recording my communication with Him. I'm a writer, so I write. (I have friend who is a photographer, so she takes pictures.) When I write, I always print "LA:" just before what I sense God saying to me. And then we go back and forth with one another. Most often we're discussing a passage of Scripture.

Sometimes God talks to me when I'm hiking or jogging or sitting on the porch that wraps around my "laughing place" in the mountains. At those times I use my voice and talk to Him as if He's sitting or walking or jogging there with me. I'm sure it would be quite funny for you to see me. I probably look like a small child who entertains her imaginary friend. I interact with the thoughts that come into my mind in response to the things I am saying. Many of my life's major decisions have been made during these kinds of conversations. At other times I just let off steam and God "takes it." I know that's not very spiritual, but it's practical and it's honest. The funny thing is that when I'm fussing I know that God listens, and sure enough at the end of my ranting and raving, conviction whispers. It's amazing how powerful that whisper can be.

While God most often speaks to us through His Word, it is possible to read, study, memorize, and live in strict obedience to the Word of God and miss the dynamic of the personal relationship He wants to have with us. This was Jesus' complaint with the Pharisees. They were teachers of Scripture. They had the first five books of the Bible memorized. In fact, they read the Scripture in the original languages and made a profession out of explaining to others the meaning of the text. But when they met Jesus, they didn't recognize Him as the Son of God. It was the greatest tragedy of Jesus' earthly life.

> When God speaks, He communicates directly to your heart.

This happens today. Many of our universities are filled with biblical scholars who do not know God personally. Some of our churches harbor a few of these. They are men and women who are more interested in arguing Scripture than they are in applying its teaching to their lives. They want to be right more than they want to be made righteous. I have an old college friend who taught religion in several Christian colleges and wrote Sunday school curriculum for a Christian publisher. Today he's living with a woman who is not his wife; his lifestyle no longer demonstrates a man set apart from the world, and church attendance is not on his agenda. He has a PhD in philosophy and religion.

Without developing the ability to dialogue with God through this intimate heart language, you may be deceived like so many other truly intelligent people are. Jesus used the analogy of sheep to explain this truth. You can read His analogy in John 10.

I met a writer who actually visited a shepherd to learn more about the habits of sheep. She discovered that sheep have quite a special relationship with the shepherd. They follow his voice, and his only. The relationship between the sheep and their shepherd must be similar to the one that Misty and I share. Their relationship is unique, personal, interactive, and special. The intimacy they share with their shepherd is built on his tender care of them. I imagine that as a sheep grows old, she deepens her trust in her shepherd if she has a good one. Through all her life's experiences, she's grown to understand that her shepherd will lay down his life before he will let harm come to her. I love the fact that Jesus said, "I am the good shepherd. The good shepherd lays down his life for the sheep" (John 10:11).

You do not serve a silent God. God speaks through His Word. God speaks through other people. God speaks through dreams and visions. God speaks through worship. And when God speaks, He communicates directly to your heart.

Oh God, Please . . .

Discussion Questions

1. Do you know any modern-day Pharisees (people who study the Bible but do not know God)?

2. How might you be careful not to become like the Pharisees?

3. Describe how God speaks directly to your heart.

Pray: *Oh Father, thank You for inviting me to have a personal relationship with You. Thank You for doing the supernatural work of transforming my head knowledge to heart knowledge. I want to know You with all that I am—my head, my heart, my spirit, my soul . . . all of me. Help me to grow in my understanding of this beautiful heart language that is our very own. Right now I'm going to be very still and very quiet so that I can listen to Your voice.* [Spend two minutes in perfect silence waiting, watching, and listening for the voice of God.]

CHAPTER 7

Test the Voice of God

The man who enters by the gate is the shepherd of his sheep. The watchman opens the gate for him, and the sheep listen to his voice. He calls his own sheep by name and leads them out. When he has brought out all his own, he goes on ahead of them, and his sheep follow him because they know his voice. But they will never follow a stranger; in fact, they will run away from him because they do not recognize a stranger's voice.

— JOHN 10:2–5

Before we leave this section of my book, I want to warn you to test the voice of God. I've told you that God speaks directly to our hearts through His Word, other people, dreams and visions, and worship. And He does. But every time God speaks, the devil tries to mimic his voice. Jesus told His listeners that His sheep will not be distracted by the voices of imposters. He said that his sheep will know his voice.

I am a child of God. I know that I am one of those sheep who Jesus mentioned when He spoke of His flock in John 10. I've been following the voice of my Shepherd ever since I was eleven years old. But there have been times in my life when I have been confused, mistaken, and even deceived. There have been times when I've fallen prey to the schemes of the enemy, and I've mistaken his voice for God's. Not only have I, at times, mistaken the voice of darkness for the voice of God, but I have also mistaken my own flesh for the voice of God. Let me explain these dangers so that you will learn how to test the voice of God and avoid making the same mistakes.

Beware of Wolves

Jesus warned that we live in a hostile environment. In keeping with the analogy of sheep, He warned of the sheep's mortal enemy, the wolf: "I am sending you out like lambs among wolves" (Luke 10:3). He also told us that those wolves might disguise themselves as sheep: "Watch out for false prophets. They come to you in sheep's clothing, but inwardly they are ferocious wolves" (Matthew 7:15).

What a terrible picture of reality! Lambs among wolves? Wolves disguised as sheep? What I love about these verses is that we serve a Lord who tells us the truth. Don't ever forget that God tells you the truth, even when the truth might not be what you want to hear.

How do these wolves attack us in our prayer lives? Consider those that are cloaked as sheep. Jesus told us that those wolves are false prophets. They use the Word of God and distort it to say what is culturally popular, or pleasant to our ears. I believe the prosperity gospel fits into this category. Anyone who preaches that yielding your life to the Lord will deliver you from all suffering is not speaking the truth. We serve a suffering Savior. How can we not expect to suffer as well?

> We serve a Lord who tells us the truth.

Anyone who lives like a king on the tithes and offerings of others ought not be trusted. How can men and women of God bathe in wealth while hundreds of thousands of people suffer and die simply because they are poor? I remind my son, who is eager to be a prosperous business leader, that if God gives him the ability to make wealth, he can be assured that wealth is to be invested in God's kingdom work. I am baffled by the number of people who flock to follow wealthy orators with a mind-set to increase their own wealth. When that person speaks, he might sound like a sheep—quoting Scripture and telling Jesus' stories—but unless His message will preach in the poorest community in any of many Third World countries, it simply is not true.

Watch out for false prophets. Jesus told us how to determine the difference between a wolf in sheep's clothing and real sheep: "By their fruit you will recognize them. Do people pick grapes from thorn bushes, or figs from thistles? Likewise every good tree bears good fruit, but a bad tree bears bad fruit" (Matthew 7:16–17).

When you are desperate to hear the voice of God, you are vulnerable to deception. False prophets might tell you what you want to hear, but temporary "ear tickles" will only lead to long-term regret. The truth is what sets you free, even when the truth might hurt. Beware of wolves.

Beware of "Vain Imaginations"

I have always considered my creative energy a good thing. But there are times when I so desperately want God to do something for me that I imagine I hear Him tell me exactly what I want to hear. Here is a for instance. After three years of infertility treatment, God allowed Tom and me to conceive our daughter Mikel. When she was born, my heart changed—a lot! I wasn't prepared for what becoming a mother would do to me. I'd been working in a ministry that I loved, and we imagined that our baby would just fit perfectly into our ordered lives. You probably know that babies and ordered lives don't necessarily go hand in hand. Pretty soon Mikel turned my life upside down and inside out. Where I once loved traveling, meeting new people, and staying in new places, I no longer enjoyed those trips. My heart yearned for the pace of life to slow so that I could enjoy time with my miracle baby.

You might think that I would have just given up my job and gone right home, but it wasn't that simple. I was making two-thirds of our family income, and my job covered our insurance. I also loved what I was doing. I'd gone to college and graduate school to have a job just like this one. So, I struggled and I prayed.

One day I was sitting in the worship service on Sunday morning, and I sensed the voice of God tell me that I was pregnant. I was going to have another baby—a boy this time—and I could quit my job. I was so sure I'd heard from God that my heart raced. I wanted to tell Tom my revelation, but I decided I'd wait and confirm my "word" with a pregnancy test, which I took the next day on my lunch hour. Unfortunately the results were not definitive. Where I was supposed to see a mark if I was pregnant, I saw only a very faint line. So, I called the doctor's office and told the nurse about my confusing test results. She encouraged me to come to the office and take a test there. The results were the same, still not definitive.

As she shook her head in confusion, she asked, "Why do you think you're pregnant? Have you missed your period? Are you nauseous? What symptoms do you have?" I felt my cheeks warm, then I looked at her and said, "I think God told me that I am pregnant." Now I wasn't nearly as sure as I'd been on Sunday. She smiled and suggested we draw blood and test it for the pregnancy hormone. She drew my blood, and I went back to work. A little while later she called me with this news: "Congratulations, Leighann, you must have heard God right; you are pregnant!"

> The truth is what sets you free, even when the truth might hurt.

I couldn't wait to tell Tom that I was pregnant, that we were having a boy, and that I could quit my job! He was thrilled with the news of our pregnancy, excited about the prospects of a boy, and not so happy about me quitting my job. It took him a few weeks to adjust to the idea, but he did.

About the time that Tom warmed up to the idea of me quitting my job, we were able to determine the sex of our baby. I was on such a faith journey that I was certain we were having that boy. When the technician assured us that we were having a girl, I couldn't believe my ears. But she was right and I was wrong. We did in fact have a beautiful baby girl who is my Kaleigh today.

You see my desire to have a boy created a bit of interference in what I heard from God. His voice did tell me that I was pregnant, and when I discovered that I could hear Him tell me something I did not know, that gave me the confidence I needed to walk away from a great ministry so that I could be a full-time mom. But my own "vain imagination" made that baby a boy.

We must be careful to submit the "voice of God," that we think we hear, to the possibility that we could mistake our wishes for His purposes. I did have a baby boy, twenty months after my second daughter. God is good, and He does love to satisfy our heart's desires, but His ways and ours are not always the same. Beware of your vain imaginations.

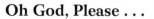

Oh God, Please . . .

Discussion Questions

1. Have you ever met a wolf in sheep's clothing? What harm did he do?

2. How can you determine the difference between a real and a false prophet?

3. Have you ever mistook the voice of God for your own vain imagination? Share that experience.

4. Does God want you to be happy more than He wants you to be holy? What is the difference?

Pray: *Lord, I long to know Your voice—to hear You when You speak and to walk in perfect harmony with You. Sometimes I don't know if I'm hearing You or me or the enemy. I get confused, and my confusion turns to doubt. When I'm not doubting You, I'm doubting my ability to hear You! I surrender my limited understanding to You. I surrender my vain imagination. I know that what You want for me is far better than what I want for myself. I trust You.*

If we want to hear God's voice,
we must surrender our minds
and hearts to Him.

—

BILLY GRAHAM

PART 2

When God Is Silent

Where is God when millions of his children are being persecuted in the most brutal ways? Why does he keep silent in the middle of persecution but speak loudly in the middle of conferences with famous speakers and worship bands? I have prayed many times like Luther: "Bless us, Lord, even curse us! But don't remain silent!"[4]

—

ZIYA MERAL

CHAPTER 8

Praying through God's Silence

O my God, I cry out by day, but you do not answer, by night, and am not silent.

— PSALM 22:2

Now that we've thoroughly discussed the mysterious "voice" of God, let's talk about what to do when that voice is silent.

I spent time yesterday with a hurting friend. She has suffered multiple losses, any one of which is plenty to grieve. Her grief is multiplied, her emotions are spent, and she confessed to me that God seems to sit silent. Having experienced some tremendous losses myself in the past few years, I can personally attest with her that the hardest part of walking in darkness is experiencing the silence of God.

In Hannah Hurnard's classic little book *Hinds' Feet on High Places*, she likens God's silence to an endless "mist."

> *At last the storm gradually died down, the clamor on the mountains ceased, and it was time to resume the journey. However, the weather had broken completely, and though the storm itself was over, thick mist and cloud remained, shrouding everything on the heights.*

When they started the mist was so thick that they could see only the trees on either side of the narrow path, and even they looked ghostly and unreal. The rest of the forest was simply swallowed up and entirely lost to sight, veiled in a cold and clammy white curtain. The ground was dreadfully muddy and slippery, and although the path did not climb nearly so steeply as before, after some hours Much-Afraid found to her amazement that she was missing the rolling thunder of the storm and even the sickening crash of the trees as the lightning splintered them.

She began to realize that, cowardly though she was, there was something in her which responded with a surge of excitement to the tests and difficulties of the way better than to easier and duller circumstances. It was true that fear sent a dreadful shuddering thrill through her, but nevertheless, it was a thrill, and she found herself realizing with astonishment that even the dizzy precipice had been more to her liking than this dreary plodding on and on through the bewildering mist. . . . At last she burst out impatiently, "Will this dull, dreary mist never lift, I wonder?"[5]

The silence of God is like a thick mist, cold and clammy, blurring your surroundings. What happens when you read God's Word and it simply does not seem to speak personally to you? What happens when the two-way conversations you enjoy with God feel as if they are going nowhere? What about those worship services that you attend where you feel like a bystander who somehow got passed over? What do you do when you pray and your prayers seem futile and God seems to be very far removed from you? These are the questions the next few chapters will answer.

What's Your Burden?

Don't you love people stories? While my husband reads hundreds of "serious" books, I personally prefer "storybooks." A most recent joy for me has been escaping to Mitford with Jan Karon's books. Mitford is a small town where everybody has a story. And, even though he isn't necessarily looking to hear them, the gentle parish priest gets caught up in most all of Mitford's people stories.

I've been a pastor's wife long enough to know that everybody has a burden. Everybody's got a heart cry! And because you are reading a book titled *Oh God, Please Help Me with My Doubt!* I am going to assume that you've got a burden—maybe more than one. What's your burden?

Most often the cries of our hearts are what press us toward God in prayer. Have you ever written your heart cry down on paper? When I wanted a baby, my prayer journal read like a broken record. "Lord, give me a child!" was the first request printed on each day's entry. God might have felt a bit pestered, but nonetheless, I just kept telling Him what I wanted.

Chances are you've talked to God about your burden, too, but you're not sure it's working. In fact, you're beginning to wonder whether He cares. What do you hope happens to this burden while you read this book? If you're the kind of reader who underlines, circles, and prints exclamation points and stars beside sentences you agree with (and I hope you are), circle all of the following statements that apply to you.

While I read this book, I want to . . .

- see this burden lifted/have this heart cry answered once and for all;
- find out why God remains silent;
- find out what I can do to speed up the answer to my prayer;
- learn how to recognize God's voice and hear His take on the situation;
- make some sense out of my life;
- find out whether God really cares, and if He does, why this is happening to me.

Even if you circled every one of these statements, you are not alone. I hear you. And believe it or not, I know what you feel. I've not experienced your exact situation, but I have struggled to somehow connect my longing to God's heart. I'm not the first one who's done that, nor are you the only one who has suffered the longing you're suffering now.

> Most often the cries of our hearts are what press us toward God in prayer.

The Bible is full of stories about real people dealing with real life. One of those people is David, and because David was a writer, we get the honor of having access to his prayer journal. Turn in your Bible and read Psalm 143.

Oh God, Please . . .

Read Psalm 143 aloud. Read it again. Now, print it in your prayer journal.

I remember the days of old;
I meditate on all Your works;
I muse on the work of Your hands.
I spread out my hands to You;
My soul longs for You like a thirsty land. Selah

—

PSALM 143:5-6 NKJV

CHAPTER 9

Begging God to Listen

*O Lord, hear my prayer, listen to my cry for mercy; in your
faithfulness and righteousness come to my relief.*

— PSALM 143:1

I f you want to learn how to pray through doubt, begin with
David's prayers. Just read them aloud and make them your
own. You will discover some surprising things about prayer
if you take time to think about his words.

Take Psalm 143:1 for instance. In just this one sentence
we can assume David might have wondered whether God was
listening at all. This prayer sounds to me as if David begged
God to "hear" his prayer—to "listen" to his cry. We can also
assume David was in some kind of anguish and he looked to
God for relief.

As David begged God to hear him, he appealed to God's
faithfulness and His righteousness. Then almost as if David
caught himself in mid-sentence, he quickly reflected on what
he'd just requested (that God respond to his heart cry with
righteousness) and asked God to exempt him from judgment:
"Do not bring your servant into judgment, for no one living is
righteous before you" (Psalm 143:2).

Recognizing Your Enemy

Be aware that you will have spiritual opposition when you
pray. In Psalm 143:3 David listed three ways the enemy was
attacking him:

1. "The enemy pursues me,

2. "he crushes me to the ground;

3. "he makes me dwell in darkness like those long dead."

Don't be caught off guard. The enemy exercises these ancient tactics against those who pray today just as he used them against David in his day.

The enemy pursues. He doesn't sit back and wait for you to engage him in battle; he is aggressive. Your enemy will get up and in your business. The enemy pursues your marriage, your ministry, your children, and your friendships—anything that you hold dear. Your enemy is constantly on a pursuit to steal, kill, and destroy all that is good in your life.

The enemy crushes God's children as often as he can. His ideal way of crushing you is to cause you to question God's goodness and to challenge His wisdom. In other words, the doubt you might be feeling could be a direct result of the enemy crushing you. He is most effective at doing this when God seems silent. Be aware that when you are living in the "meantime" (that time that exists between your desperate need and God's faithful provision), you are vulnerable to the enemy's attack. And if you give into the doubt the enemy dangles in front of you, your spirit will be crushed. We will talk more about specific doubt in future chapters.

> Your enemy is constantly on a pursuit to destroy all that is good in your life.

Once he crushes your spirit, the enemy will make you feel as if you are dwelling in darkness like those long dead. Although you might be in good company (with David), you don't want to remain in this place. To dwell in darkness like those long dead is to be caught in a place of despair—without hope, without faith, without light, and without God. I've been there; have you? I fall into that place when I let my enemy crush me.

When Prayers Seem Ineffective

I cannot help but believe that some of David's despair in this prayer was a result of his feeling as if God was ignoring him. And while we could possibly come up with 101 spiritual remedies to feeling this way, I have to confess that even the most powerful prayer warriors—including all the great "heroes" of the faith—felt this way at one time or another.

Look closely at the description of David's despair:

→ David felt crushed to the ground.

→ He felt like living was as desperate as death.

→ David declared his spirit faint and his heart dismayed.

I read these verses and want to shout encouragement to David—to tell him it will get better and that this won't last forever. But at the same time I read these verses and want to thank David for being so honest and real. In a way, David gives me permission to struggle when I pray—to wrestle with my faith and whine a bit when the circumstances of my life stand in absurd contrast to the abundance I heard Jesus describe in John 10:10.

Continue reading Psalm 143, and discover how David dealt with God's seeming silence . . .

Did you find it?

When God seems silent and your prayers ineffective, take time to remember. David said, "I remember the days of long ago; I meditate on all your works and consider what your hands have done" (Psalm 143:5).

Remember When . . .

I cannot possibly write to you specifically, for I don't know you. But I can prompt you by sharing where my memories might take me. I remember when I was lonely and longing for a life companion, someone to love who would love me—someone who loved God and understood my call to ministry.

I remember when my life companion left me at home almost every night of the week to visit the people in our community when we were building our tiny congregation. I remember the quiet house and how empty it felt. I remember walking through the baby aisles in the local discount market and dreaming of the baby I longed to have as my very own.

I remember when I lost my son at Disney World and wondered if life as I knew it was about to come to an end and I'd never be the same again. I remember hearing that my daughter was pregnant (through the gossip mill in our small community) and begging God to make it not so.

You get the idea. Try it! Choose memories that desperation created. Think back to days when you were crushed in spirit and your heart was dismayed. But choose memories that are distant, because God did a great work to make them reasons to rejoice. And when you remember, meditate on all God's works; consider what His hands have done.

I remember meeting Tom McCoy at Southwestern Seminary in Ft. Worth, Texas, and I will never forget the August evening when he got down on one knee in the wet grass at the

Dickson County Country Club in his Tennessee hometown and asked me to be his wife.

I remember the lunch hour I took to drive downtown to my infertility specialist's office and take a pregnancy test—how the two nurses and receptionist who were eating their lunch in (and who knew all the treatment I'd endured for three grueling years) celebrated my miracle with me.

I'll never forget four-year-old T.J. seeing me at the entrance to the souvenir shop beside Pooh's ride at Disney World after we'd been apart for more than twenty eternal minutes, and the way his eyes lit up and his little legs ran toward me as I fell to my knees and reached out to him.

And just today I've held my beautiful granddaughter in my arms and soaked in the pure joy of her laughter.

It's good to remember—both the despair and God's work. Then, after you have remembered, choose God. Once David remembered—after he meditated on all God's works and considered what God's hands had done—he said this: "I spread out my hands to you; my soul thirsts for you like a parched land" (Psalm 143:6).

David remembered that God is able. He reached his arms heavenward, stretched his hands open, and begged God to do what He was able to do in his life.

Oh God, Please . . .

Discussion Questions

1. Have you ever felt as if you were pursued by the enemy? What did that feel like? What did you do about it?

2. Has the enemy ever crushed you? Describe that experience.

3. Share some of your desperate memories.

4. How did God meet some of those desperate needs?

Pray: *Oh God, I know that You are able. I remember how You . . . [talk to God about something He did for you in the past]. Thank You for answering my prayer then. I was so desperate and so eager to experience You. With the memory of how You met me then, I ask that You meet me today. I yield to You my heart's desire and I trust You. Because I see how You worked in my past, I trust You today to do the same in my future.*

CHAPTER 10

Begging Is OK

I spread out my hands to you; my soul thirsts for you like a parched land.

— PSALM 143:6

There is no shame in begging. If there were I think God would have edited David's prayer. There is nothing gained by doubting, but there is no shame in begging.

David determined to turn to God for relief; he described how desperately he needed relief, then he begged God to give him relief quickly:

> *Answer me quickly, O Lord; my spirit fails. Do not hide your face from me or I will be like those who go down to the pit. Let the morning bring me word of your unfailing love, for I have put my trust in you. (Psalm 143:7–8a)*

David didn't want to wait forever for God to answer his prayer. He didn't pray for perseverance or patience; he prayed for God to give him relief. Sometimes we cloak our lack of faith with a super-spiritual posture of praying for perseverance and patience when really the reason we pretend we are OK with God's silence is because deep down inside we don't really expect Him to answer.

I am afraid that I don't have much patience with prayers that end with the phrase "Lord willing." Of course we ought to pray for the Lord's will to supersede our own when we come to Him with our requests. I've written much on the necessity of surrender in this mysterious partnership we have with God that we call prayer. Often, however, people insert the phrase "Lord willing" to give God an "out." Just in case He's not willing—or just in case absolutely nothing happens in response to their prayers. I am frustrated with the phrase because it might often mean, "What difference does it make if I pray or not?"

This is not what David did. When David prayed, he remembered God's activity in the past and begged Him to "do it again" in his present. In fact, he got quite specific in his request: "Let the morning bring me word of your unfailing love." David cried out to God in his despair and begged Him to answer his prayer by the next day. I like that kind of praying!

Faith-building Prayer

The great thing about praying as David prayed is that your faith is bolstered. I imagine that if I could take a poll of every reader of this book, most of you would agree that God is faithful. Most of you would also agree that His love is unfailing. But, like the man who brought his son to the disciples, we desperately need God to prove His faithfulness and His unfailing love in our lives *right now*.

The story is found in Mark 9:14–27. A man brought his son to Jesus' disciples because an evil spirit possessed the boy. Unfortunately Jesus' disciples couldn't drive the spirit out. Jesus was away at the time, and when He returned, a large crowd had gathered for a theological discussion.

Seeing the crowd, Jesus asked what they were arguing about. The father told him how awful life was for his boy and how Jesus' disciples failed to help. Jesus rebuked His disciples for their lack of faith then focused His attention on the boy. As the evil spirit acted out, the boy's father prayed, "If you can do anything, take pity on us and help us" (Mark 9:22b).

Jesus heard the father's desperate plea and picked up on one tiny, two-letter word: *if.* "'If you can'?" said Jesus. "Everything is possible for him who believes" (v. 23).

And then the father responded with one of the most honest prayers I've ever heard: "I do believe; help me overcome my unbelief!" (v. 24).

How many of us, if we were really honest, pray as this dad did. "I do, believe, Lord, but please help me with my doubt." My favorite part of this story is the next part. Jesus helped this dad with his doubt by answering his prayer. I love that!!

Just like the father who brought his son to Jesus, we also really *know* that God hears our prayers, is intimately acquainted with our grief, and that He has the power to solve our problems when He shouts answers to our heart cries.

> The great thing about praying as David prayed is that your faith is bolstered.

I knew God was faithful when the nurse at Dr. Daniel's office (my infertility specialist) read the results of my pregnancy test and said, "Leighann, you are pregnant!" I experience God's unfailing love every time my precious granddaughter lays her head on my shoulder and smiles up at me, and I wonder why I ever begged Him to not let her be.

It's one thing to profess a distant belief in the faithfulness and love of a faraway God but quite another to experience His faithfulness and love as it intersects your desperate heart cry. It is quite all right to beg God to answer your prayers quickly. Begging is OK.

Oh God, Please . . .

Discussion Questions

1. What might happen if you asked God to answer your prayer by tomorrow morning?

2. How might you have felt had you been one of Jesus' disciples the day that father brought his son for help?

3. How might God help you with your doubt today?

Pray: *Oh Jesus, I do believe! Help me with my unbelief! I have this need* [tell Him all about it], *and I desperately need You to help me.*

CHAPTER 11

Begging with Resolve

Teach me to do your will, for you are my God; may your good Spirit lead me on level ground.

— PSALM 143:10

Just as David begged God to answer his prayer quickly, his tone shifted from one of desperation to a tone of submission. Can you find the phrases that indicate this shift? Read Psalm 143:8–12.

How about these?

➤ "for I have put my trust in you. . . .
➤ "for to you I lift up my soul. . . .
➤ "for I hide myself in you. . . .
➤ "for you are my God; . . .
➤ "for I am your servant."

Notice that David made these resolves before God ever responded to his prayer. Unlike people I know who've given God ultimatums then turned their backs on Him when He failed to meet their requirements, David declared his resolve.

> *Lord, I put my trust in You. I don't have a plan B. If You don't come through for me, I will still trust You. You are worthy of my allegiance; I've given my life to You, so it is in You I trust.*
>
> *Lord, I lift my soul up to You. Here I am, desperate with nowhere else to turn. I*

will not look around for relief. I won't go outside the parameters of Your Word. I won't take matters into my own hands. For to You I lift up my soul.

Father, I hide myself in You. You are my only safe place. I have no other refuge. I've put all my confidence in Your ability to protect me, to answer my cry, and to get me out of this mess.

You are my God, and I am Your servant—way back then when things were going my way, right now when they are not, and in the future when I don't have a clue what will come. You are my God, and I am Your servant.

When you beg, beg with resolve.

If you read carefully, you can also see how David's prayer evolved. At the beginning of this prayer, David begged God to deliver him (verses 1, 7–8), but in verses 8–10, he prayed:

➻ "Show me the way . . .
➻ "Teach me to do your will . . .
➻ "Lead me on level ground."

Feel free to beg God for answers, but when you do, resolve to trust Him, to wait on Him, to hide yourself in Him, to follow Him, and to serve Him. In the meantime, walk in God's ways. Be a diligent student of His will, and follow Him on level ground. (To walk on level ground is to let the Word of God lead your way. Don't let your emotions pave your path. When you give your emotions free reign, you will find yourself straining the scale of the rocky heights one day, only to be hurled over the edge the next. When God's Word leads your way, you will walk on level ground.)

The Reason We Pray

Much of our desire for prayer is motivated by a desire for change, and most likely the change we are looking for is a change in someone or something else. We want our husbands to be more loving or our children to be more Christ-centered. We want our work to be more productive or our bank accounts to be more cushioned. We want health

> God brought David to a deeper understanding of his privileged position with His Creator.

and wealth, and the list goes on and on. But how self-centered and small-minded are we to think that the God of the universe sits on His throne just waiting on us to give Him a "to-do" list?

David wanted change. More specifically, he wanted relief. I don't know what was going on, but apparently he had either an internal spiritual attack or an external enemy attack and he longed for peace. But as his prayer unfolded, God brought David to a deeper understanding of his privileged position with His Creator and Lord.

And that is what prayer does. Read Psalm 143:10–12. Notice how David's prayer evolved. As David asked God to change his circumstances and his enemies, God in turn changed David. He was consumed with what was happening around him, but God turned David's attention to what was happening within him (and above him).

Oh God, Please . . .

Discussion Questions

1. Does David sound like the boy who took Goliath down in this Psalm? How do you think that he went from that place to this one?

2. What causes your faith to wane and your doubts to increase?

3. What resolves might you make in your life today?

Pray: *Father, like David I am resolved to be Your servant, to follow You, and to trust You. Please come to my aide, relieve me of my doubt, and answer me when I pray. Give me a glimpse of Your power today.*

PART 3

Five Keys to Delete Doubt from Your Prayer Life

Professing Christianity has taken the true doctrine of prayer and made it into a pious, self-righteous ritual. The shrieks and cries of sweaty, circus tent-sized "prayer meetings" have turned prayer into a spectacle. And those who pray the "gimmes" treat God as though He was a genie in a bottle. They only call on Him when they want something, usually for selfish reasons. This is not what God intended.[6]

—

DAVID C. PACK

CHAPTER 12

Key 1:
Base Your Appeal
to God on the Relationship

In your unfailing love, silence my enemies; destroy all my foes, for I am your servant.

— PSALM 143:12

"Hear my prayer, O Lord!"

How could a man after God's own heart be so desperate to be sure God was hearing his prayer? God loved David. David wrote most of the psalms. David prayed all the time. It would be easy to assume David . . .

* never got burned out;
* never felt like his prayers went nowhere;
* never *wondered* whether God was there;
* never grew distressed over unanswered prayer.

But Psalm 143 gives us indisputable proof that when David penned *this* prayer he was exactly where we find ourselves all too often today: burned out, helpless, wondering, distressed, and doubting. However, as we studied this Psalm in the previous chapters, we discovered that David didn't give up hoping that God would come through for him. As David prayed he gave us five keys to unlock spiritual doors, doors locked by doubt, which separates us from God's heart. God called David a man after His own heart because he possessed these keys. In this chapter you will discover the first of these keys then apply it to your situation.

David Recognized Who He Was in God's Sight

Look again at Psalm 143. Read verse 2. What does David say about himself?

- ❧ I am Your servant.
- ❧ I am unrighteous.

The first KEY to doubtless prayer is:
You must base your appeal to God on your relationship with Him.

At the beginning of this prayer, David appealed to God on the basis of his relationship with Him. Consider the relationship David had with God. You'd have to take time to read each of the following stories to get the full impact of the depth of David's relationship with God, but here is a brief overview.

In 1 Samuel 17:45–50 David killed Goliath because he was passionate about defending the name and reputation of God. Ironically, David made a name for himself that day, but his intent was to exalt the name of God.

In 1 Samuel 23:1–5 David bravely chose obedience to God even when he met resistance from his own men. Not once but twice David asked God whether he should go fight the Philistines, and although his men were afraid, David obeyed God and fought the Philistines.

In 1 Samuel 24 David waited for God to give him the throne he'd been promised rather than taking matters in his own hands and securing the throne for himself. David's submission to God's timing was perhaps one of the greatest examples of the depth of his relationship with God.

> David didn't give up hoping that God would come through for him.

David's servant relationship with God was built on faith. David believed in the goodness of God. David's servant relationship was built on obedience. David obeyed God's commands. And finally, David's servant relationship was built on trust. David trusted God.

Are you God's servant? Do you believe in the goodness of God? Do you obey Him? Do you trust God?

Oh God, Please . . .

Discussion Questions

1. Which of the following sentences might describe the relationship you have with God?
    - I am His servant.
    - I am His child.
    - I am God's acquaintance.
    - I am God's bond-slave. (A bond-slave is a former slave whose freedom has been purchased, but because of her love for the master, she chooses to remain in his service.)

2. Why did you choose your particular descriptive word?

3. What is your relationship with God built on?
    - Faith: I believe God is good, and I trust Him.
    - Hope: I know God exists, and He rewards those who seek Him. I have placed *all* my hope in Him.
    - Love: I know God loves me, and I love Him; therefore, I trust Him.

4. How does your view of your relationship with God impact the way you pray?

Pray: [Father, Master, Lord, God], please hear my cry! Answer me in Your faithfulness, in Your righteousness! I am Your [child, servant, acquaintance, bond-slave]. Therefore I am asking You to . . .

CHAPTER 13

Key 2:
Base Your Appeal to God
on His Righteousness

There is not a righteous man on earth who does what is right and never sins.

— ECCLESIASTES 7:20

Many people make the mistake of bringing God their merit as if by doing so they can convince Him that they are deserving of His favor. They present to Him all their good deeds, they compare themselves to others, and then they present their requests to Him. God is not impressed with our good deeds.

The second KEY to doubtless prayer is:
You must base your appeal to God on His righteousness
and not your own.

David recognized who he was in the sight of God. Look at Psalm 143:1–2.

> *O Lord, hear my prayer, listen to my cry for mercy; in your faithfulness and righteousness come to my relief. Do not bring your servant into judgment, for no one living is righteous before you.*

Notice David's train of thought. "Oh God, listen to my cry for mercy; You are faithful. You are righteous. Please come to my relief. Oh . . . but don't judge me in Your righteousness, for no one living has any right to even stand before You. I am Your servant, but I am also unrighteous."

I Am Unrighteous

David recognized who he was in the sight of God. He'd already appealed to God's faithfulness and His righteousness in verse 1. I like to picture David on his knees crying (physically) out to God. As soon as the word *righteousness* left his lips, I see David quickly catch his sobs and stop for a moment. Then, as he realizes what he's just said, I think David quickly adds verse 2: Oh, yeah. But God—deal with *them* according to Your righteousness, not mine. I *know I'm not righteous*!

Even though David wanted God's righteousness to rule in his circumstances, his heart was pricked with the inescapable truth that *if* God ruled in righteousness, he (David) would have to be dealt with according to that same holy righteousness! Thus, the plea: "Don't judge me; I'm Your servant! And I know that no one is righteous, not even me." Here David humbles himself before God.

Romans 3:10 repeats Ecclesiastes 7:20: "As it is written: 'There is no one righteous, not even one.'"

When I was infertile, I prayed: "Oh God, please! Look at all those teens who are getting pregnant and aborting their babies. Look at those women in Third World countries who birth eight, nine, and ten babies and can't even afford to feed them! Why me?! Why can't I have just one little child?!"

Do you hear the subtle way I tried to appeal to God according to *my righteousness* rather than His? In my mind, I was much more worthy than those women. I *deserved* to have God answer me. I failed to realize that I needed to follow the example David gave us in Psalm 143:2 and appeal to God according to *His righteousness* rather than my own.

The Holiness of God

In today's culture we don't practice worship in secular terms. When I think of being *bowed down*, I am reminded of a scene from a motion picture, *Anna and the King*. In this scene the king enters the courtyard, and everyone falls to their knees with their faces to the ground. Only one remains standing: Anna. The king's counselor asks, "Who *is* this woman who considers herself equal to a man?" The king replies, "Not equal to a man, but equal to a king!"

Please listen to me carefully here. Too often we experience frustration, despair, and unanswered prayers because we fail to bow down. Somehow, in our misconstrued thinking, we are like Anna in the king's presence. We come to God as if we are His equals! We appeal to Him based on *our* righteousness.

> Too often we experience frustration, despair, and unanswered prayers because we fail to bow down.

Lest I offend you, consider how you might have done (or be doing) this. What reasons have you given God to convince Him you *deserve* answers to your prayers? Think about this, and review your prayers. If those reasons you've offered to God have more to do with you and your qualifications than they have to do with God, then you need to recognize that you have based your prayer on your righteousness rather than God's.

Isaiah 64:6 says this: "For all of us have become like one who is unclean, and all our righteous deeds are like a filthy garment" (NASB).

My righteous deeds (giving my tithes, teaching Sunday school, going to seminary, leading the children's worship, spending time with my own children, biting my tongue, and controlling my anger) are stained by sin and therefore no more than a filthy garment to a holy God! I can *never* base my prayers on my merit.

So, what then do we base our prayers on? The same things David based his prayers on in Psalm 143.

KEY 1:
We must base our appeal to God on
our relationship with Him.

KEY 2:
We must base our appeal to God on
His righteousness and not our own.

Oh God, Please . . .

Discussion Questions

1. How have your prayers reflected thoughts of your own righteousness?

2. Consider and describe the holiness of God.

3. How does thinking about the holiness of God impact the way you pray?

Pray: *Lord, I realize that I have been appealing to You based on my own righteousness. I've felt like I deserved Your answer because . . . Please forgive me for doing this. Help me to understand what David knew, that if You dealt with me on the basis of my righteousness, I would be judged perhaps severely. Thank You for making provision for my unrighteousness through Your Son, Jesus Christ.*

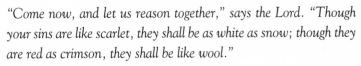

CHAPTER 14

Righteousness That Is Yours

"Come now, and let us reason together," says the Lord. "Though your sins are like scarlet, they shall be as white as snow; though they are red as crimson, they shall be like wool."

— ISAIAH 1:18

I n the previous chapter we determined that we have no righteousness apart from God. The truth of our unrighteousness is hard to swallow. I don't know about you, but I don't like to think that my righteousness is like a filthy garment to God. If our righteous acts are like filthy rags to God, what then are we to do?

Yesterday we discovered that David humbled himself before God and appealed to God's mercy by pleading with Him: "Do not bring your servant into judgment, for no one living is righteous before you" (Psalm 143:2). Remember that David lived prior to Jesus' coming. David's faith in God was based on his knowledge of God's character, and His belief that God would send His Savior (see Psalm 22). Through Samuel God anointed David to be king of Israel and put His Spirit on him (see 1 Samuel 16:1–13). David, just like us, had no righteousness before God, but he had a heart for God. Because David trusted God's character and his heart was genuine, God's mercy covered David's unrighteousness. See Psalm 51 for a glimpse of how the Spirit of the Lord convicted David of sin.

Like Abraham, Moses, Joshua, and the other men of God before him, David was justified by faith in God and His *coming* Messiah. Although David and others lived before Christ's sacrificial death, they will meet us in heaven. Their faith in God and His coming Messiah covered their unrighteousness and healed their sin.

What Righteousness Is Available to Us Today?

We, however, live on this side of the cross of Christ. We are not like David. We don't live in hope of what is to come. We live by faith in what has already come. Let me explain this way. Look again at Isaiah 64:6. According to this verse we are condemned before a *holy* God. Now read Isaiah 1:18. According to this verse, a *loving* God has a plan to take away our condemnation: "'Come, let us discuss this,' says the Lord. 'Though your sins are like scarlet, they will be as white as snow; though they are as red as crimson, they will be like wool'" (HCSB).

Notice that Isaiah quoted the Lord saying, "They *will* be." Jesus fulfilled that *will*. Today, God doesn't say, "They *will be*"; today He says, "They ARE!" Look what happens when we rewrite Isaiah 1:18 changing "they will be" to "they are": "'Come, let us discuss this,' says the Lord. 'Though your sins are like scarlet, they *are* as white as snow; though they are as red as crimson, they *are* like wool.'"

Praise God we live after Jesus fulfilled God's will. Romans 5:6–10 explains how Jesus' sacrifice made the way for us.

> You see, at just the right time, when we were still powerless, Christ died for the ungodly. Very rarely will anyone die for a righteous man, though for a good man someone might possibly dare to die. But God demonstrates his own love for us in this: While we were still sinners, Christ died for us. Since we have

now been justified by his blood, how much more shall we be saved from God's wrath through him! For if, when we were God's enemies, we were reconciled to him through the death of his Son, how much more, having been reconciled, shall we be saved through his life!

I love to lead others through the process of receiving Jesus' offer of salvation. First I show them Romans 3:23, where we all stand condemned in the sight of God; and second, Romans 6:23, where we realize the wages of sin is death. Not only are we condemned but we are sentenced to death. And then comes that wonderful three-letter word *but*—perhaps the best "but" in the entire Bible! *But* the free gift of God is eternal life in Christ Jesus our Lord. So, we don't have to remain condemned. We have a Savior!

It's like being in a courtroom. You are the accused. There is no jury, only the righteous Judge. There is no appeal process; what He decides is final. The sentence for your crime is death. You have nowhere else to turn. Your defense attorney presented every bit of evidence he could: you are a good person, you helped people, you attended church, and you even gave money! You were honest, you put your family first, and you were a generous friend and a loving mother . . .

The Judge lifts His gavel to declare His verdict, and to your surprise, He slams the

> Because David trusted God's character and his heart was genuine, God's mercy covered his unrighteousness.

gavel down and shouts, "*Enough!*" Then He looks at you with eyes of such compassion you can't look away. His love for *you* fills His entire being. The Judge looks at the hundreds of thousands sitting in the gallery waiting for their time in your seat, for they stand accused as well. And He weeps—hard, soul-wrenching sobs. His crying is so loud that His Son enters from the chambers and kneels at His Father's feet. The Judge holds His Son's face in His hands, and as tears splash on the face of His beloved Son, He says, "It is time." The Son solemnly nods in agreement and quietly rises to leave. You and the others are dismissed as the Judge goes alone to His chambers.

You wonder what just happened, when you hear angels singing, "Glory to God in the highest / And on earth peace among men with whom He is pleased" (Luke 2:14 NASB). "And the Word became flesh and dwelt among us, and we beheld His glory, the glory as of the only begotten from the Father, full of grace and truth" (John 1:14 NKJV).

Making the Application

Jesus' mission to earth was for one primary purpose: to reconcile men once and for all to God. He fulfilled that purpose with steady intent. Jesus directed His eyes toward the cross. When you have some time to ponder this, read the record of His last days in Luke 22–23.

Because of what Jesus did, my courtroom trial will go something like this. I sit in the seat of the accused; the righteous Judge sits on His throne; beside Him sits His Son. When my time comes, the Judge looks at me then looks at His Son. Jesus rises, walks to where I'm sitting, wraps His strong arms of salvation around my shoulders, and says, "Father, she's mine." To which the Father/Judge smiles with deep relief and says, "Welcome Leighann, enter into My rest."

How do I know this is so? Because Romans 10:9–10 tells me that I must do two things in order to be saved: "That if you confess with your mouth Jesus as Lord, and believe in your heart that God raised Him from the dead, you will be saved; for with the heart a person believes, resulting in *righteousness*, and with the mouth he confesses, resulting in salvation" (NASB, emphasis added).

So, what about our righteousness before God? My friend, the good news is that *if you have believed in the Lord Jesus Christ—in your heart—you have been reckoned as righteous before a holy/loving God!* You are no longer condemned!

So, how does this apply to the second key to prayer? *Base your appeal to God on His righteousness, not your own.*

If you have personally applied Romans 10:9–10, you can pray in the confidence that you are approaching God as righteous because Jesus is making intercession for you. But be careful to continue to humbly understand that your righteousness is not your own. Your righteousness was made possible by the sacrificial death of God's beloved Son, initiated by the righteousness and love of God. So, you must still base your appeal to God on *His* righteousness provided to you through *His* Son Jesus Christ.

Oh God, Please . . .

Discussion Questions

1. Have you personally applied Romans 10:9–10 to your life? If you have, then share what a difference this has made.

2. How does this discussion of righteousness impact the way you pray?

If you have not personally applied Romans 10:9–10 to your life, consider praying this prayer. Print it in your own words in your prayer journal.

Dear God,

I know I am a sinner. I believe Jesus died to forgive me of my sin. I repent and turn from my sin. I accept Your forgiveness and the gift of eternal life. Thank You for forgiving me and for my new life. I want to follow and obey You in all I do.

Pray: *Oh God, thank You for letting Jesus die so that I could live. Thank You for redeeming my life. Thank You for the righteousness that You have given me. I am humbled to think that I can approach You boldly in righteousness because of the sacrifice of Christ. Today, I lift my request to You, not because there is anything in me that thinks that I deserve an answer, but because Your involvement in my life will demonstrate Your glory. Thank You for giving me boldness when I pray.*

CHAPTER 15

Righteousness and Relationship

For you have not received a spirit of slavery leading to fear again, but you have received a spirit of adoption as sons by which we cry out, "Abba! Father!" The Spirit Himself testifies with our spirit that we are children of God.

— ROMANS 8:15–16 NASB

In the previous chapter we discovered that when we receive Jesus as our Lord and Savior, we are "reckoned as righteous" before a holy God. Our righteousness is no longer as a "filthy rag" to God. Our sins are no longer red as crimson. They *are* (not *will be*) white as snow. Praise God that we can bring our requests boldly to Him as children of righteousness!

In this chapter we will examine the impact that Christ's mission of reconciliation has on our relationship with God. If you have your Bible with you, read Romans 8:1–17.

What Is Your Relationship with God?

Because Christ fulfilled God's mission of reconciliation, those who receive Jesus' death on the cross as a substitute for the death they deserve, now stand innocent before a holy God: "Therefore, there is now no condemnation for those who are in Christ Jesus, because through Christ Jesus the law of the Spirit of life set me free from the law of sin and death" (Romans 8:1–2).

In relationship with God, you once were guilty but now you are innocent.

Romans 8:3–4 tells us that the law explained and defined sin. The law refers to the standard of holiness set forth in the Old Testament. While the law could help us understand God's expectations, it was powerless to save us from our sin. No way existed that we, in our sinful nature, could ever fulfill the law to God's standard of perfection. So, God sent His own Son to fulfill the requirements of the law and to be a sin offering for us (see Romans 8:3). God saw fit to allow His Son to serve as a substitute for us so that He could die and we could live.

Through the tremendous gift of His own Son, God took away sin's power to condemn us. Because Jesus was the perfect sacrificial Lamb of God, His offering for sin condemned sin, rendering sin powerless to separate us from God. According to Romans 8:4 those who live according to the Spirit are no longer powerless under the weight of sin; they are free from sin's power—free to live a new life in step with the holiness of God.

In Romans 8:5–8 we learn the difference between a person walking according to the sinful nature and the person who walks according to the Spirit. It's all a matter of what goes on in your head: "Those who live according to the sinful nature have their *minds set* on what that nature desires; but those who live in accordance with the Spirit have their *minds set* on what the Spirit desires" (Romans 8:5).

Is it possible to determine what you set your mind on? YES! It is possible to choose what comes in and out of your mind. Which is easier? To change your thoughts or to change your feelings? The heart is a bit harder to tame, where the mind can be guided and directed. We make thousands of choices daily. We either "go with the flow" and let the world, and others, make our decisions for us, or we make our decisions intentionally based on our goals, passions, and convictions. The mind is a powerful thing—so powerful that we can actually think ourselves into new ways of feeling. The mind, empowered by God's Spirit, can choose to deny natural desires and live in accordance with the Spirit.

According Romans 8:6–8 "what the sinful nature" desires and the desires of the Spirit are polar opposites. Note the following phrases regarding the mind-set of a sinful man:

⇒ "The mind of sinful man is death, . . .
⇒ "the sinful mind is hostile to God.
⇒ "It does not submit to God's law, nor can it do so.
⇒ "Those controlled by the sinful nature cannot please God."

Compare those phrases to the powerful statement regarding the mind-set of a Spirit man: "The mind controlled by the Spirit is life and peace" (v. 6b).

Considering the serious repercussions of living according to the sinful nature as opposed to living by the Spirit, Romans 8:9 is an encouraging word! "You, however, are controlled not by the sinful nature but by the Spirit, if the Spirit of God lives in you. And if anyone does not have the Spirit of Christ, he does not belong to Christ."

> Through the tremendous gift of His own Son, God took away sin's power to condemn us.

If you have received Jesus as your Savior—if you have submitted your mind, your heart, and your everything else to His Lordship—then you are no longer controlled by the sinful nature that leads to death. You are now under the control of the Spirit of God, and your mind is filled with life and peace. If your mind is not filled with life and peace, then your problem is not in your prayers but in your relationship. Right now, talk to God about your relationship, and let Him show you what adjustments need to be made.

Romans 8:10–17 continues spelling out the difference between living a life controlled by sin and living a life controlled by the Spirit of God.

→ "your body is dead . . . yet your spirit is alive
→ "the Spirit . . . [gives] life to your mortal bodies
→ "live according to the sinful nature [and] you will die
→ "live . . . by the Spirit [and] you put to death the misdeeds of the body"

As you walk and live in harmony with God's Spirit, you become His sons and daughters. You begin to look like Him, to talk like Him, to embrace His perspective on life. When you cry out to Him, you do so from the intimacy of a child who is eager to have a deep bond with her Father. And because of the intimacy you share, you can literally call God "Daddy" (*Abba* translated means daddy).

From My Heart to Yours

I pray that God has opened your minds to understand these verses. Paul put the flesh versus Spirit struggle in language the common man of that day could understand. This entire discourse might have resulted from someone saying something like this to Paul: "I decide every morning that today will be different! I want to do what is right. But then, before the children are even out the door for school, I've already done what comes naturally. And bad stuff just comes out of me! I am enslaved to my flesh!"

To which Paul's response is: "Christ did away with sin's power over you! Don't walk according to the flesh, walk according to the Spirit which lives in you!"

Satan wants you and me to think that we are powerless to control our fleshly appetites. Satan wants us to be defeated. Defeated Christians are one of His greatest tools. He makes a mockery out of our defeat. He points his accusing finger our way and says: "See there?! God didn't come through on His promise to you! Your own flesh is more powerful than God in your life. *You*, even without my picking on you, are overcome by sin! Sin is stronger! Sin will keep you down! The things written in the Bible were for the super Christians in a time God was *really* working. They are not for today." And with that he skips away, laughing at the defeat he used to plant seeds of doubt, despair, and condemnation.

What Paul said in Romans 8:15–17 is your best defense against this kind of defeat. Personalize these verses like this:

> I did not receive a spirit that makes me a slave to fear, I have received the spirit of sonship [daughtership]. I can cry out, *Abba! (Daddy!)*, *Father!* My Father's Spirit testifies with mine that I am indeed His very own daughter [son]. And because I am His, all that is His is mine. I will inherit everything that is good and rich and abundant and glorious because I am a child of the King. I will suffer, just like my big brother Jesus suffered before me, but out of that suffering I will share in His glory.

Do you hear the victory of these verses? Satan tries to get you to believe you are alone and defeated by your own flesh! He knows the power of flesh. But God, who knows you best and loves you perfectly, also knows the power of your flesh. He says you are His! You are His son. You are His daughter. You are not a common man. You are not an ordinary woman. When you received God's free gift of salvation through Jesus Christ His Son, God gave you more than eternal life; He made you His. He calls you His own. He adopted you to be His children!

The next time Satan comes at you with his bundle of deceitful lies, you shout at the top of your fleshly lungs: "GET BACK FROM ME, YOU LYING SERPENT! I AM NOT DEFEATED. I AM A CHILD OF THE KING OF KINGS AND LORD OF LORDS. I AM HIS, AND HE WILL SEE ME THROUGH!"

So, how does this study apply to key 1? *We must base our appeal to God on our relationship with Him.*

Do you remember what word you used to describe your relationship with God? The best word to describe our relationship with God is "child." If you have received God's gift of salvation—confessed with your heart Jesus as Lord and believed in your heart that God raised Him from the dead—you are His child! Every heart cry you lift may be based on your relationship with God, and that relationship is as a child to his or her loving Father. But don't think of your earthly Father when you think of God. Think of a Father who has all wisdom, all power, and perfect love. That, my friend, is our Father. That is our King. He's the one we have been given the privilege of calling "Daddy, Lord."

Oh God, Please . . .

Discussion Questions

1. How does Romans 8:1–17 affect your understanding of God's great love for you?

2. Do you know for certain that you have received God's gift of salvation? Have you asked God to forgive you of your sin and understood that Jesus died so that you could live? If not, talk to God about that right now!

3. Share with one another the difference you've experienced in your life as you've grown to understand that you are no longer under sin's control.

Pray: As you pray today, realize you are talking with your Father who loves you. You are not hoping to make a fuzzy connection with some unreachable cosmic power. You are drawing near to your perfect Father. Picture God sitting in your favorite armchair, and crawl into His lap.

Oh Daddy, I am so sorry for being lazy and choosing not to do the hard work of "putting to death the misdeeds of my body." I will do this now. [Talk to God about the behavior that you participate in that you know is not in harmony with Him.] *Thank You for loving me and for giving me life by the power of Your Spirit. Help me to understand what victory is mine as I learn to walk according to Your Spirit.*

CHAPTER 16

Key 3:
Face and State
the Reality of Your Situation

The enemy pursues me, he crushes me to the ground; he makes me dwell in darkness like those long dead. So my spirit grows faint within me; my heart within me is dismayed.

— PSALM 143:3–4

We've already determined that David wrote Psalm 143 at a time when he was desperate to hear from God. In verses 3 and 4 David stated the reality of his situation. Because David was in such a dark and desperate place, the devil took full advantage of him. Notice the specifics of the attack. The enemy pursued him, he crushed him, and he made David dwell in darkness ("like those long dead"). David didn't dress up his prayer, use the King James Version, or attempt to sound holy. Basically he said, "I'm hurting here, Lord; are You listening?"

David faced the reality of his situation, and he honestly presented it to God. This is the third key David hands us from Psalm 143: *Face and state the reality of your situation.*

Many people think that they have to dress up their prayers so that they can present them to God. God already knows more about your heart than you do. When you pray, He wants to show you what He knows is already in there. You can never tell God anything that He doesn't already know. There's no reason to beat around the bush when you come to God in prayer. The most powerful prayers are the most honest prayers.

Why God Delays

In this prayer, David cried out to God in complete honesty. He faced and stated the reality of his situation, and the reality was that Satan was taking full advantage of God's silence. Sometimes Satan comes at us from this angle: "If God really loved you, He'd relieve your pain. At the least, He'd give you some kind of reassurance that He's listening to you. But look at you, God is gone and you're hurting."

Have you ever felt like you were dwelling "in darkness like those long dead"? I have.

How could David—the man after God's own heart, filled with the Spirit of God—get himself

> The most powerful prayers are the most honest prayers.

into such a desperate situation? When you find yourself in a place like this, step back from your present circumstances so that you can get a broader perspective on what God might be doing in your life.

Let's look for a moment at the early days of David's public life. We meet David in 1 Samuel 16. There we discover that David was the youngest son of Jesse, and he was ruddy and had beautiful eyes and a handsome appearance (1 Samuel 16:11–12). He was God's "chosen one," the next in line to be king of Israel. God directed Samuel to anoint him in response to God's rejection of Saul as king. David was a shepherd. As far as we know, he didn't aspire to such a position. Unlike Joseph, who dreamed of his brothers one day bowing down to him, we find no evidence that David had ambitions of one day being a great ruler.

I, for one, assume that because God sought out David, sent Samuel to anoint him, and gave David His own Spirit as a guide, David would enjoy a peaceful celebrative journey to the throne. After all, David didn't ask God for this honor. But, God did not give David the throne right away. God told Samuel that David was king, and Samuel told David. No one, however, told Saul, and, therefore, David was the object of Saul's jealous anger. This was not because David flaunted his position but rather because Saul knew the Spirit of God had departed from him.

How did Saul know this? Saul had experienced the powerful presence of God (when he was first anointed king), and he knew the difference between God's presence and His absence. If you've walked with God for any length of time, you know what Saul knew. He no longer had the anointing of God on his life, and he also recognized God's presence with David. Deep down inside, Saul knew that David was destined to take his place. I don't know whether Saul actually believed he could interrupt God's purposes, but being the rebellious man he was, he did everything within his power to kill David before he could take the throne. David never threatened Saul. He never cheated him, challenged him, or tried to take his throne from him. But David had to run, hide, fight in self-defense (all the while saving Israel from her enemies, the Philistines), and resist the temptation to kill Saul and put himself out of his misery. You can read this story as it unfolds in 1 Samuel 17–31.

The Reality of the Situation

Finally, the Philistines critically wounded Saul, and he took his own life. But then only part of the throne was passed to David. Second Samuel 3:1 says this: "The war between the house of Saul and the house of David lasted a long time. David grew stronger and stronger, while the house of Saul grew weaker and weaker."

War continued between the descendants of Saul and the "house" of David. It might have been during this time that David penned Psalm 143. Can you imagine how exhausting David's life had been? First he was attacked by Saul simply because God chose him to be the next king. Then, after Saul's death, rather than a smooth transition of rule and reign, David suffered continued conflict with Saul's family.

But notice that something happened to David throughout this struggle. *David grew stronger.*

While the house of Saul grew weaker, David grew stronger. Here is another truth I will give you for God's silence to our prayers and His delays in answering our heart cries: *Sometimes God delays in answering our prayers because He is strengthening us for His kingdom's work.*

While David might have wondered whether God was listening to his prayer, God was tenderly watching and carefully measuring David's strength of character. God chose David to be His king, and while David might have considered these battles *his* unanswered heart cries, they were not that at all. The battles were the Lord's training ground for the enormous responsibilities and challenges that would come with God's choosing David for greatness. God's mission was simple: He was turning a shepherd boy into a king.

Remember how I told you that the Bible heroes were only ordinary people with extraordinary faith in God? Don't miss this very important truth: *They were no different than you and me!* David's heart was soft and teachable. He sought God while he was a shepherd, but David was an ordinary person. Being a shepherd was only a very little bit like being a great king. Shepherds take care of sheep. Kings take care of kingdoms. God knew the difference, so God took a shepherd with a right heart and created just the right training program to make him the greatest king Israel ever knew.

God wants to do the same with you. The unanswered prayer that is fueling your doubt might be your customized training program because God has big plans for *you*!

Let's never forget that some of God's greatest mercies are His refusals. He says no in order that He may, in some way we cannot imagine, say yes. All His ways with us are merciful. His meaning is always love.

—

ELISABETH ELLIOT

Oh God, Please . . .

Discussion Questions

1. How does the devil fuel your doubt when God is silent? What thoughts does he plant in your mind?

2. Imagine you are David's wife, and you've watched him suffer through Saul's attacks. And now that Saul is dead, Saul's descendants are still against your husband. What would your prayers sound like?

3. If you've ever suffered through a season of God's silence but then been rewarded by position and responsibility, share that experience with your group.

Pray: Print Jeremiah 29:11–13 in your prayer journal. This is God's word to you today. Ask Him to show you how it applies specifically in your situation. Don't be afraid to write what God reveals to you.

Lord, I know that You have specific plans for my life. I choose to believe Your Word when it tells me that these plans are for my good and not to harm me. But right now I'm living in a situation that seems quite different than the plans You've promised. Please open my eyes so that I can see from Your viewpoint. Help me to see the bigger picture so that my endurance is renewed.

CHAPTER 17

Satan's Tactics

Be self-controlled and alert. Your enemy the devil prowls around like a roaring lion looking for someone to devour. Resist him, standing firm in your faith, because you know that your brothers throughout the world are undergoing the same kind of sufferings.

— 1 PETER 5:8–9

David was discouraged by God's delay in answering his heart cry. Satan used this period of delay to step into action. The result? David felt as if he was living in a grave with decomposing bodies! I'm going to give you one ingenious insight you will forever be thankful for: Satan is *not* creative. He is smart, powerful, and completely evil, but he is *not* creative. Once you figure out his few tactics, you are way ahead in fighting him off.

> Satan knows what we forget . . .

But, hear me say this as well: although Satan is not creative, he is crafty! He will consistently look for ways to defeat you with his effective, though uncreative, tactics. I've written a book called *Spiritual Warfare for Women* where I talk much about the extent and limitation to Satan's power. For the purpose of dealing with doubt, however, let's take a quick look at Satan's tried-and-true tactics. They are outlined best in Genesis 3:1–7.

Tactic 1: Question God's Word

We meet Satan when he encountered Eve and asked this question: "Did God really say, 'You must not eat from any tree in the garden'?" (Genesis 3:1).

Did Satan know the answer to this question? Was he concerned with God's instructions? Yes and no. Satan knew that God's instructions were that Adam and Eve could eat from all the trees in the garden except the one, and he was not the least bit concerned about God's instructions. Satan knows what we forget, and that is that God's instructions lead to life and peace and blessing and everything we need to live in favor with Him and with others. But, because he is intent on undermining God's purposes and His plans, Satan uses questions to stir up doubt.

Tactic 2: Question God's Character

Eve was not immediately snookered; she responded to the serpent's question with truth: "We may eat fruit from the trees in the garden, but God did say, 'You must not eat fruit from the tree that is in the middle of the garden, and you must not touch it, or you will die'" (Genesis 3:2–3).

The only reason Satan asked Eve about *all* the trees was to set her gaze on the one tree that God declared "off limits." Once he had her attention focused on what she could not have, Satan went to work challenging God's character and His motives: "'You will not surely die,' the serpent said to the woman. 'For God knows that when you eat of it your eyes will be opened, and you will be like God, knowing good and evil'" (Genesis 3:4–5).

Satan, in essence, calls God a liar. Was God a liar? Did He mislead Adam and Eve? Were His words not true? Better questions might be these, Is God a liar? Has He ever misled you? Have His words ever proven not to be true?

I've spoken in a lot of churches across our nation, and when I speak to an audience that has a lot of older women in it, I like to ask these questions: "Have any of you ever experienced a time when God has been unfaithful to you? Has He ever not kept His Word in your life?" As often as I ask those questions, I've never discovered anyone who has declared God to be less than faithful nor His Word less than true.

The problem comes when we grow shortsighted. The serpent was right; Eve didn't die *right away*, at least not physically. But the minute she ate the forbidden fruit, Eve's relationship with God was severed; spiritually she died. And later, because she ate the fruit, Eve physically died. We've all been dying since. God spoke the truth when He told Adam and Eve that if they ate the fruit from the tree of good and evil they would die.

The serpent was also correct about Eve's eyes being open. As soon as she ate the fruit from the tree of knowledge, her eyes were open to evil. Before she took that bite, her eyes were only open to good. In a way she knew more than she did before, but what a terrible knowledge! I see many young people make this same mistake today. They refuse to listen to the voices of reason, experience, and love and instead turn away from the biblical values they were taught as children. In some attempt to be their "own" person, they choose evil over good. Certainly their eyes are open, eventually, but most of them grow to regret gaining that kind of knowledge.

Do you see how Satan subtly calls God a liar then uses truth, twists it, and plants seeds of doubt in Eve's heart? Satan urged Eve to consider God's motives for His rules. He didn't say it, but he implied that God didn't want Eve to be like Him, that God wanted to lord over Eve by giving her restrictions in her life that would cheat her out of the complete experience.

Satan pitched God not as a loving companion but as a strict authoritarian. What makes me mad is that he uses this same tactic today and people still fall for it.

Satan made it seem that God forbade Adam

> You are responsible not only for your own behavior but also for the way you exercise your influence.

and Eve to eat of the fruit for His good rather than theirs. Satan placed seeds of doubt in Eve's heart. Examine the doubt that you are wrestling with today. What thoughts have you considered? Do any of them sound like these questions that Satan presented to Eve? If they do, then you can be sure that the devil is trying to steal blessing from your life. Don't let him do this.

Tactic 3: Hit 'Em with the Flesh! (While Their Defenses Are Down)

The Bible tells us why Eve chose to eat the fruit that God told her not to eat. Her disobedience was not a random mistake but a well-thought-out, intentional decision to go her own way rather than God's. Read Genesis 3:6 and see if you can find three reasons Eve ate the fruit: "When the woman saw that the fruit of the tree was good for food and pleasing to the eye, and also desirable for gaining wisdom, she took some and ate it. She also gave some to her husband, who was with her, and he ate it."

1. She saw the tree was good for food. (Her taste buds wanted it.)
2. She saw the tree was pleasing to the eye. (She liked the way it looked.)
3. She saw the tree was desirable for gaining wisdom. (It promised to deliver something she'd never experienced before.)

Satan used Eve's fleshly desire for physical pleasure and power to entice (tempt) her to sin.

A Sideline Gender-sensitive Discussion

Guys, don't miss the fact that verse 6 does not say Adam happened to walk by at that moment, after Eve had already eaten the fruit. Neither does the Scripture say that Eve dressed the fruit up in a salad, and unbeknownst to Adam he ate it. The verse says, "She also gave some to her husband, who was *with her*, and he ate it" (emphasis added). Adam stood silently by and watched his "woe man" make a bad choice.

Where was his spiritual leadership and authority? Where was his conscience? Why did he let her eat first? Was she the guinea pig? "I'll just wait and see if Eve dies, then if not, I'll eat too!" Oh, Adam.

Satan was strategic in engaging Eve and not Adam in conversation. Peter told husbands to exercise great consideration and respect in regard to their wives, calling them "the weaker partner" (1 Peter 3:7). Satan targeted Eve because she was more likely to give in to his persuasive tactics. This should be a wake-up call to both men and women.

Men, while Satan was tempting Eve, he was after Adam. Satan was set on the fall of Adam. Only in the fall of Adam was Satan successful in stealing God's perfect creation from Him. He knew the amazing power of persuasion that women

have over men. Satan knew how strong their influence could be, so he strategically put Eve between him and Adam in order to bring Adam down. This ought to be a sober warning to you. Be careful which women you allow to influence you, and be on guard against women who might influence you to disobey God.

Husbands, you are told to love your wives as Christ loves the church. When you stand silent and watch your wife fall miserably, you will be called into account for her. Christ will one day present the church to God beautiful and whole. The day will come when you will be standing before the throne of God, and God will expect you to give an account for your wife. Christ wants you to present your wife to God beautiful and whole. Perhaps you've already watched your wife fail miserably. Please don't be discouraged. Just begin to do the right thing now. Be your wife's strong support. Let her know you care and that she doesn't have to walk alone. You may be surprised at just how much your effort toward support and love will encourage her. Beg God to teach you how to love your wife as Christ loves the church.

Women, solemnly recognize the power of influence you have over the men in your lives. While Adam answered to God, so did Eve. You are responsible not only for your own behavior but also for the way you exercise the powerful gift of influence you have over your husbands, sons, fathers, and all other men in your lives.

How This Applies to Your Heart Cry

Has Satan engaged you in conversation by using God's delays in answering your prayers? Has he whispered . . .

- ❧ "God's not interested in you. If He were, why isn't He talking?"
- ❧ "Did God really say you had to die to the flesh? You can't do that!"
- ❧ "If He were out there, He'd make Himself known! He's not there."
- ❧ "If He cared, He'd do something about this. He doesn't care."
- ❧ "If He were listening, He'd let you know it! He's not listening."

Have you ever heard any voices like that? I have. And it doesn't really matter how educated we are, how long we've been saved, or how many people we've "led to the Lord." I gave my life to Jesus when I was eleven years old. I've served on numerous mission trips and church staffs. I've been a children's minister, youth minister, education minister, prayer minister, and women's minister. I've served as a camp counselor at more than one camp; I've directed Christian camps and served as a statewide church consultant. I've been a curriculum writer and prayer retreat leader. I was educated at a Christian college and a Southern Baptist seminary. I even married a pastor. But I still hear that slithery whisper. It makes the skin on the back of my neck crawl. And too often I listen.

Oh God, Please . . .

Discussion Questions

1. What part of Satan's interaction with Eve makes you the most angry?

2. Have you experienced Satan's lies up close and personal? If you are willing, share your experience with your group.

3. Have you discovered ways that you can overcome Satan's voice? Share these with your group.

Pray: *Lord, if I were truly honest with You, I would confess that I've heard that serpent too. He just gets in my head and messes with me! He tells me that there are other ways to live and still be pleasing to God—that I don't have to give up the things of this world. He questions the harm. He makes me feel like the Bible is full of rules and that if I follow them I'll be missing out.*

Besides that I know a lot of Christians who are sad people. I don't want to be sad. But neither do I want to bring death into my life. I want to live, Lord. I want to live my life pleasing to You and filled with the adventure of following You every step of the way. I know people who love You. They are full of peace and joy and energy. I want to be like them.

I trust You, Lord. Even when You are silent, just like David I will appeal to You—not to any other—and I certainly will not give heed to Satan's slippery tongue.

CHAPTER 18

Key 4:
Base Your Appeal
to God on the Ways
He's Worked in the Past

I remember the days of long ago; I meditate on all your works and consider what your hands have done.

— PSALM 143:5

In Psalm 143, David shows us how we can pray in the midst of God's delays and Satan's attacks. By doing so, he gives us the fourth key to praying through God's silence: *Base your appeal to God on the ways He's worked in the past.*

David's Response to God's Delay and Satan's Attack

David remembered the days of long ago; he meditated on all God's works and considered what His hands had done. Here David gives us a valuable tool to dig ourselves out of the pits of despair. When we are faced with doubt and Satan has targeted us for attack, we must remember where we've been and what God has done for us. If we find that difficult to do, we must look at the work of His hands and marvel at His greatness! We can imitate David and do three distinct things when we pray:

1. "I remember the days of old" (v. 5a, NASB)

Oh, to journey in those memories. The little shepherd boy watching over his sheep when suddenly a lion snatches a helpless lamb. The mama sheep shouts the alarm, and David grabs his slingshot! His heart races, and he runs toward the predator! Upon seeing the fierce lion (have you ever tried to take a lamb from a hungry lion?!), David calls on the name of God: "Lord, have mercy on me, Your servant! Save this little lamb!" David sends the rock hurling, and the lion falls over dead. Impossible!

Nothing is impossible with God. Then David prayed, "Thank You, Lord. Thank You. You heard my cry and answered my call." David sang as he took the lamb out of the mouth of the dead lion and gave it unharmed to its mother.

Often the psalmist went further back than his own life experience. He told of God's marvelous acts in freeing the Israelites from Egyptian bondage (see Psalm 136). If you are in such a desperate place that you cannot see what God has done for you, look at what's He's done in history! Remember the days of old. It's better to remember your own olden days, but if you cannot, just remember the times in history when God has intersected mankind with His love.

2. "I meditate on all Your doings" (v. 5b, NASB)

David meditated on *all* God's doings: the lions, the bears, Goliath, the anointing, the battles, Saul and his unpredictable temper, the wives, the victories, the failures, Jonathan, the Philistines. The list could go on and on and on. David reflected on all of his relationship with God up to this point, and the reflection encouraged David.

How long has it been since you meditated on God's doings in your own life? Can you recall specific ways God directed you? Can you think of times when God felt very near to you?

What about the times when He seemed far away? Do you remember desperate prayers that were answered with "YES!"? And those prayers you are glad He answered, "NO!"?

Meditating on all God's doings is quite a good doubt deterrent. Meditating on all God's doings will help you gain a glimpse of His bigger picture for your life. Take time right now to think of ways God's been working in your life. Write your reflections in your prayer journal. Be sure to thank God for making Himself known to you through these circumstances.

3. "I muse on the work of Your hands" (v. 5c, NASB)

David "mused" on the work of God's hands. Muse means to ponder, contemplate, and reflect upon. When smacked with the spirit of doubt and despair, David contemplated God's creation. As an example of David's musing, read Psalm 65:5–13. Look at all the aspects of creation that David pondered in these verses: the mountains, the seas, even the turmoil of the nations; the rising and the setting of the sun; the land, rain, streams, and crops (specifically grain); the overflow of the harvest, the grasslands and the desert, the meadows and the flocks.

> Meditating on all God's doings is quite a good doubt deterrent.

Have you ever been so confused, depressed, and discouraged that you could not even think straight? When you feel this way, follow David's lead: muse on the work of God's hands. Take time now to praise God for His creation. Where Satan is not creative, God is! He is the Master Creator! Muse on His creation right now. Follow the example of Psalm 65:5–13.

Victory Is with God

Although David was discouraged by God's silence and beaten down by Satan's attack, He resolved to look only toward God for his relief. David refused to look elsewhere. Because David remembered the days of old, meditated on his relationship with God, and mused/contemplated God's greatness as revealed in His creation, David reached toward God for victory: "I stretch out my hands to You; / My soul longs for You, as a parched land" (v. 6, NASB). After taking the time to remember, to meditate, and to muse, David drowned his doubt in the sea of fact.

- Fact: God loves you . . . very much.
- Fact: God hears you when you pray . . . He's heard you before.
- Fact: God has power to help you . . . His power created this world and all that is in it.
- Fact: _____
  _____ [You fill in the blanks.]

Can you honestly tell God you are stretching out your hands to Him for deliverance! Or, are you still seeking answers elsewhere? Have you come to the place where you realize that without God your situation is hopeless? Have you recognized your incredible need for Him? Yes? Tell Him so.

Oh God, Please . . .

Discussion Questions

1. Share one story that you remember from your own "days of old" that tells of God's answer to your prayer.

2. Read Psalm 65 aloud. Add other aspects of God's creation that you want to praise Him for making.

3. What part of God's "doings" do you want to "muse" on today? Share these wonders with one another.

Pray: *Father, my heart is burdened because* [tell God what burdens your heart most today]. *Nevertheless I will trust You. I trust You because I can see evidence of Your power when I look around me. I trust You because You've come through for me before* [tell Him about a specific time when He answered your heart cries]. *I trust You because You rule in righteousness and love. You have always ruled this way, and You always will. Oh God, I am burdened, but I choose to trust You.*

CHAPTER 19

Key 5:
Base Your Appeal
to God on His Character

*The Lord is gracious and compassionate; slow to anger and rich
in love.*

— PSALM 145:8

Today we will complete our study of our model "Oh
God, Please" prayer as presented by David in Psalm
143. For the sake of review, let's list the four keys David presented us in this prayer.

- ✦ Key 1: Base your appeal to God on your relationship
  with Him.
- ✦ Key 2: Base your appeal to God on His righteousness
  and not your own.
- ✦ Key 3: Face and state the reality of your situation.
- ✦ Key 4: Base your appeal to God on the ways He's
  worked in the past.

As David wrapped up this prayer, he revealed the fifth key
to doubtless prayer: *Base your appeal to God on His character.*

David's Concluding Plea

In Psalm 143:10–12, David's heart spilled over with requests,

> *Teach me to do your will, for you are my God; may your good Spirit lead me on level ground. For your name's sake, O Lord, preserve my life; in your righteousness, bring me out of trouble. In your unfailing love, silence my enemies; destroy all my foes, for I am your servant.*

Teach me	Direct me	Lead me
Bring me out of trouble	Revive me	Meet me
Silence my enemies	Rescue me	Destroy all my foes

Read Psalm 143:10–12 again. This time look for the reasons David gives God for doing these things.

> *v. 10: Teach me to do your will, for you are my God; may your good Spirit lead me on level ground.*
>
> *v. 11: For your name's sake, O Lord, preserve my life; in your righteousness, bring me out of trouble.*
>
> *v. 12: In your unfailing love, silence my enemies; destroy all my foes, for I am your servant.*

David based his final appeal to God on God's character. David acknowledged God's goodness ("your good Spirit"), His reputation ("your name's sake"), God's righteousness, His unfailing love, and the fact that God was his Master ("for I am your servant"). If you watch the progression of David's prayer, in verse 7 you see his prayer move from a place of desperation:

> *Answer me quickly, O Lord; my spirit fails.*
> *Do not hide your face from me*
> *or I will be like those who go down to the pit . . .*

to one of expectation in verses 11 and 12:

> *For your name's sake, O Lord, preserve my life;*
> *in your righteousness, bring me out of trouble.*
> *In your unfailing love, silence my enemies;*
> *destroy all my foes, for I am your servant.*

Once David contemplated God's goodness, His unfailing love, His righteousness, and His reputation, David realized that God was trustworthy. God could not let David down because God would not be God if He didn't respond to David's prayers out of His character.

Character is *who* you are. What you do comes out of who you are. You and I can pretend to be someone we are not, but eventually the pretense will fade and our true selves will filter through. The enemy might cloak God's goodness—His love, His power—by making you think that God's silence is indicative of His negligence. The devil might sneer at God's delays, and he might even point to circumstances that are impossible to understand and challenge the love of God. But God listens and responds when you pray, and if you will hold on long enough you will live to see God's character filter through the devil's shadow—and eventually that shadow of darkness will be consumed in the light of God's goodness.

Using David's Keys When You Pray

David didn't use these keys to unlock the heart of God. God's heart is not locked though at times it might seem to be. Romans 8:31–32 says this, "What, then, shall we say in response to this? If God is for us, who can be against us? He who did not spare his own Son, but gave him up for us all—how will he not also, along with him, graciously give us all things?"

We know that God is for us because He gave His own Son to ransom our lives from the grave. And because He was willing to give His own Son's life in exchange for ours, it is certain that He will graciously give us all things. God initiated giving in His relationship with us. He is *THE Giver*! When David used these keys, he didn't reach heavenward and twist them into locks on the chambers of God's heart. No! Instead, David reached deep within his own desperate heart and carefully placed these keys into the locks on the doors of his faith, trust, hope, and joy. David realized that in order to know God's power in his life, he had to open his heart wide to God. We must love God with a whole heart!

> If you will hold on long enough you will live to see God's character filter through the devil's shadow.

If doubt has swallowed your faith, then apply these keys David presented to us. But don't apply them to the seemingly locked chambers of God's heart—instead, apply them to the locked chambers of your own heart. Use these keys to unlock a faith that believes Romans 8:37–39: "No, in all these things we are more than conquerors through him who loved us. For I am convinced that neither death nor life, neither angels nor demons, neither the present nor the future, nor

any powers, neither height nor depth, nor anything else in all creation, will be able to separate us from the love of God that is in Christ Jesus our Lord."

Go ahead, use David's keys. Read Romans 8:37–39 aloud, and rejoice in a God who promises to give to you freely *all* things!

No, in all these things we are more than conquerors
through him who loved us. For I am convinced that
neither death nor life, neither angels nor demons,
neither the present nor the future, nor any powers,
neither height nor depth, nor anything else in
all creation, will be able to separate us for the love
of God that is in Christ Jesus our Lord.

—

ROMANS 8:37–39

Oh God, Please . . .

Discussion Questions

1. Romans 8:37 says we overwhelmingly conquer. Is there something in your life, or in the life of someone you love, that needs to be overwhelmingly conquered?

2. Are you willing to use David's keys to unlock those rusty doors in your heart?

3. Are you willing to take God at His Word and believe?

Pray: *Lord, I believe that there is nothing that can separate me from Your love. I need You to overwhelmingly conquer this impossible situation in my life.*

Talk to God about your specific situation, be sure to . . .

Base your appeal on your relationship with Him: *Father, I am Your child! A co-heir with Jesus and recipient of Your amazing grace.*

Base your appeal on His righteousness and not your own: *I come boldly to Your throne of grace clean before You because my sins were washed away by Your Son. I plead with You both humbly and boldly on behalf of the righteousness that is mine through Christ.*

Face and state the reality of your situation. Be straightforward and honest!

Base your appeal on the ways God's worked in the past: *Lord, I am asking You to "do it again" as You did when . . .*

Base your appeal on God's character: *For Your name's sake, and to demonstrate Your goodness, please . . .*

I am Your servant; I believe; help my unbelief. In Jesus' powerful and precious name, I pray. Amen

CHAPTER 20

Moses, Twelve Spies, and a Bad Report

Then Caleb silenced the people before Moses and said, "We should go up and take possession of the land, for we can certainly do it."

— NUMBERS 13:30

In the past several chapters, we've discussed five keys David gave us in Psalm 143. When we use these keys, we can delete doubt from our prayer lives. The five keys are these:

1. Base your appeal to God on your relationship with Him.
2. Base your appeal to God on His righteousness and not your own.
3. Face and state the reality of your situation.
4. Base your appeal to God on the ways He's worked in the past.
5. Base your appeal to God on His character.

In this chapter, you will see how Moses applied these keys in his prayer life years before David was born. If you grew up attending church as a child, you will remember the story of the spies who were sent on a surveying trip. Twelve of them went into the Promised Land to bring back a report to the Israelites who were camped on the edge of the Jordan River, which separated them from their destiny. Ten of the spies returned with a bad report, and two of them returned with a good one. This caused quite a ruckus in the Israelite camp and led Moses to pray a powerful prayer using the five keys we've discussed. But before we journey through that story, let's gain perspective by doing a little background research. If you have your Bible with you, turn to Exodus 33.

One Very Special Prayer Partner

Moses probably had the most unique prayer life of any biblical character. In Exodus 33:11 we learn that he actually spoke with God. The book of Exodus records many conversations between Moses and God. During lots of those prayer times, Moses served as the go-between (intercessor) between God's chosen people and God. During one of these conversations, Moses complained to God, "You tell me to lead these people but you haven't told me who will go with me. You tell me I've found favor in Your sight, then please teach me your ways so that I might know you better and find favor with you." (I've taken liberties; this is a loose translation of Exodus 33:12–13.)

God answered Moses with assurance that His own presence would go with Moses, and that He God would give Moses rest (Exodus 33:14). But this wasn't good enough for Moses. Moses explained to God that if that presence did not go with *all* the people then he didn't want to go forward one more step.

This is the part I especially like: "How will anyone know that you are pleased with me and with your people unless you go with us? What else will distinguish me and your people from all the other people on the face of the earth?" (Exodus 33:16). Moses knew that the *only* thing that separated the people of God from all other people (on the face of the earth) was the presence of God! We would do well to remember that fact today. Too many churches think programs, committee meetings, worship styles, and marketing plans separate the people of God from all other people. May it never be! The ONLY thing that separates the people of God from all other people is God's presence.

God was pleased with Moses' request, and He assured Moses that He would go with all of them. And I especially love the next part, too, because Moses sensed he was on a roll, so he just kept asking for more: "Then Moses said, 'Now show me your glory'" (v. 18). As close as Moses was with God, he still longed for more. The Lord explained to Moses that He would let Moses glimpse His glory, but that he would have to hide in the cleft of the rock and that God would cover him with His hand until His glory had passed—the human body was no longer able to live in the presence of God's glory (see Exodus 33:17–23).

A bit later, God put Moses in the cleft of that rock, covered him with His hand, and proceeded to proclaim His glory: "And he passed in front of Moses, proclaiming, 'the Lord, the Lord, the compassionate and gracious God, slow to anger, abounding in love and faithfulness, maintaining love to thousands, and forgiving wickedness, rebellion and sin. Yet he does not leave the guilty unpunished; he punishes the children and their children for the sin of the fathers to the third and fourth generation" (Exodus 34:6–7).

This is the revealed glory of God.

God then promised to do some specific things because His presence would remain with His people. Here are some of the things God said He would do (see Exodus 34:10–11):

- ➤ "I will do wonders never before done in any nation in all the world.
- ➤ "The people you live among will see how awesome is the work that I, the Lord, will do for you.
- ➤ "I will drive out before you the Amorites, Canaanites, Hittites, Perizzites, Hivites and Jebusites."

When God's presence is with us, the evidence of His presence will be obvious! We won't have to defend God; we won't have to create opportunities for Him. When His presence is with us, we will see Him perform wonders in our midst. But the one thing I want you to remember is what God revealed about Himself. Moses would lean on this revelation at a critical time in Israel's future. Watch to see how the story unfolds. Turn to Numbers 13 in your Bible.

Two against Ten

In obedience to God's instructions, Moses chose twelve men (one from each tribe of Israel) to go into the Promised Land and bring back a report. So, Moses chose: Shammua from the tribe of Rueben, Shaphat from the tribe of Simeon, Caleb from the tribe of Judah, Igal from the tribe of Issachar, Hoshea from the tribe of Ephraim, Palti from the tribe of Benjamin, Gaddiel from the tribe of Zebulun, Gaddi from the tribe of Manasseh, Ammiel from the tribe of Dan, Sethur from the tribe of Asher, Nahbi from the tribe of Naphtali, and Geuel from the tribe of Gad. (Hoshea was Joshua, Moses' aide.)

> When God's presence is with us, the evidence of His presence will be obvious!

He sent them with specific instructions: "Go up through the Negev and on into the hill country. See what the land is like and whether the people who live there are strong or weak, few or many. What kind of land do they live in? Is it good or bad? What kind of towns do they live in? Are they unwalled or fortified? How is the soil? Is it fertile or poor? Are there trees on it or not? Do your best to bring back some of the fruit of the land" (Numbers 13:17–20).

After a while, the men returned to give their report. However, ten of them forgot two very important facts somewhere between the time they were appointed and the time they returned.

1. Ten spies forgot who sent them.
2. Ten spies forgot what they were sent to do.

Moses sent the twelve spies to explore the land, land that God had already promised to them. It was not their assignment to determine *if* the Israelites *could* conquer the land—there's no *if* in God's purposes! The spies were appointed to initiate the beginning of God's partnership with His people in strategizing the hows to conquering the land.

You see, because God loves us, and longs to be *one* with us, He chooses to bring us in on the adventure. He could have conquered the entire land by Himself and handed it to the Israelites. But He wanted to work with them in establishing them as a mighty nation in the land. God didn't need the spies' opinion as to how difficult the land would be to conquer. He wanted their partnership in bringing the people along on the exciting victory He'd already promised.

Before we go too hard on the spies, let's look at how this might apply to our own lives, lest we miss an important lesson here. How often have we surveyed a situation and declared it impossible then whined about the hopelessness of it all. Whining, examining, taking into account the size of our enemies—all these things fuel our doubt. And doubt can keep us wandering in the wilderness.

Through the years, the church my husband leads has grown. There was a season of our church's life when we built buildings every three or four years. Every time we counted the cost of the next building project we had anywhere between 140,000 to more than 10,000,000 reasons not to build. However, with every dollar we didn't have, people within walking distance of our facility weren't being reached. We overcame those obstacles and built those buildings. Along the way there continued to be impossible prices to pay for impossible buildings to build and impossible land to acquire from impossible neighbors who didn't want to sell.

Today, God continues to magnify Himself among us by increasing our numbers both here and around the world. He continues to radically rearrange our lives to reflect His glory. But now He has us in impossible places to reach (some via foot paths and boats) among impossible languages to learn. We have ongoing ministries in many Third World countries and unreached people groups.

All along the way we need to be like Joshua and Caleb, the two spies who

- remembered who sent them;
- remembered what they were sent to do.

Eventually Joshua and Caleb led God's army years later when the Israelites finally got to enter the Promised Land. The people of Israel provide us with a perfect example of what not to do when you're faced with impossible circumstances.

Back to the spies: Once the men returned from their scouting trip, Moses and Aaron assembled the whole community for the report. The scouts showed the people the fruit and validated the truth that the land did indeed flow with milk and honey. *But* . . . with that three-letter word, the spies proceeded to tell their fellow countrymen how big and powerful the people were and how impenetrable their cities seemed to be.

In essence, they could have said something like this. "Look at what God has done to us. He's led us to this Promised Land; it is just as fertile and desirable as He said it would be. In fact, it is all that God promised and more. But, why would He do this to us? The land is filled with giants. The giants are much bigger than us, and their cities will be impossible to capture. We cannot have the Promised Land of God as long as those giants are there. Not only that, but we are much smaller and certainly no match for them. Look at what God has done to us."

Have you ever felt that way? Perhaps you feel that way now. Did God answer your prayers for children just to give you children that are breaking your heart? Did God answer your prayers for a ministry only to seemingly abandon you in that ministry, turning you over to naysayers and persecutors? Have you ever experienced the seeming contradiction of God? Nothing like the impossible to breed doubt and sprout despair.

Oh God, Please . . .

Discussion Questions

1. Can you relate to the experience of the Israelites? If so, share that experience with your group.

2. Why is it hard to trust God when you are faced with giants?

3. What might have happened to the children of Israel if they had chosen to trust God? What might happen for you when you choose to trust God?

Pray: *Lord, it would be easy to read this story and pretend that I'd be like Joshua or Caleb, the spies who trusted You. But too many times I let the "giants" in my land swallow up my faith. I tend to focus on my circumstances and forget Your promises. Show me how I might be doing this now. Remind me of Your promise regarding my situation. Thank You, Lord, for giving me Your Word. I believe You will keep it.*

CHAPTER 21

Doubt Breeds Despair

That night all the people of the community raised their voices and wept aloud.

— NUMBERS 14:1

The bad thing about negative thinking is that it tends to be contagious. Fear spread among the Israelites much faster than faith: "All the Israelites grumbled against Moses and Aaron, and the whole assembly said to them, 'If only we had died in Egypt! Or in this desert! Why is the Lord bringing us to this land only to let us fall by the sword? Our wives and children will be taken as plunder. Wouldn't it be better for us to go back to Egypt?' And they said to each other, 'We should choose a leader and go back to Egypt'" (Numbers 14:2–4).

What Did the Israelites Do?

➤ Their doubt gave way to fear, and their fear pummeled them into pandemonium. They cried for themselves: "If only we had died in Egypt! Or in this desert! Why . . . ?"

➤ They grumbled against their leaders: "We should choose a leader and go back to Egypt."

➤ They questioned God's character and motives: "Why is the Lord bringing us to this land to let us fall by the sword?"

➤ They rebelled against their leaders: "We should choose a leader and go back . . ."

If you are not careful, your doubts might send you down this same slippery slope.

Consider David's keys: What did the Israelites forget?

1. They forgot their relationship with God. Of course the Lord didn't bring them to the edge of the Promised Land just to heckle them with the possibilities and abandon them to the giants! He would never do that!

2. They completely disregarded His righteousness. The Israelites were right and they were wrong. They were right in wondering why God would abandon them to the giants in the land. There was no way that God's righteousness would leave them in such a lurch. Had they remembered the righteousness of God, they would have known they'd drawn the wrong conclusions.

3. They didn't factor God into the reality of their situation. By themselves, the Israelites were most certainly defeated by the inhabitants of the Promised Land. But with God they could take those giants down! At the outset of their journey (in Exodus 33), Moses had already established that God would always go with them. Joshua and Caleb were the only ones who factored God into the reality of their situation.

4. They chose to forget what God had done for them in the past. God set the Israelites free from Egypt with the ten plagues; He parted the Red Sea, drowned the Egyptian army, fed the Israelites while they were in the desert, led them through the wilderness . . . For goodness' sake, they experienced firsthand the "doings" of God that David still remembered years later in his prayers. But they chose not to remember what God had done for them in the past. They behaved as if they had never seen the mighty working of a powerful God.

5. They misjudged the character of God. After all this time in the desert—being fed by God, protected by God, led by God, and loved by God—the Israelites still didn't really *know* God. They based their understanding of God on a wrong assumption. They assumed God was cruel, unjust, and out to get them. They were suspicious, ungrateful, rebellious, full of pride, and void of faith.

In order to understand and experience God at work in and through your life, you have to embrace a foundational truth. We say it often in our worship services: *God is good, all the time. All the time, God is good.*

When you wrap your heart around that basic truth, you will consider God's involvement in your life through eyes of faith. You will seek and experience the goodness of God even in the midst of the most impossible situations!

Oh God, Please . . .

Discussion Questions

1. It's easy to see where the Israelites went wrong, but does this ever happen to you? Have you ever been faced with an impossible situation and given in to doubt and despair?

2. Which of the five keys are you most likely not to use?

3. Which one of the five keys is most important?

Pray: *Oh God, so many times I let my circumstances color my faith rather than letting my faith color my circumstances. It's so much easier to be one of ten than one of two. But Lord, I want to be one of those who chooses to place my confidence in You. I want to believe that You are bigger than anything I might face. I want to want to experience You do what only You can do, and I know that means I might have to face a few giants.*

CHAPTER 22

A Faithful Few Believed

Moses said to the Lord, . . . "Now may the Lord's strength be displayed, just as you have declared."

— NUMBERS 14:17

In contrast to the doubtful, fearful, and frantic response of the Israelites, Moses turned to the Lord in prayer. He and Aaron, Joshua, and Caleb gave us an example of what to do when order becomes chaos. While the bad report of the spies spread through the camp (don't forget that each man was strategically chosen so that he could communicate to his own tribe), the tribes came unglued. The heat was rising and the atmosphere for mutiny was inevitable.

> *Then Moses and Aaron fell facedown in front of the whole Israelite assembly gathered there. Joshua son of Nun and Caleb son of Jephunneh, who were among those who had explored the land, tore their clothes and said to the entire Israelite assembly, "The land we passed through and explored is exceedingly good. If the Lord is please with us, he will lead us into that land, a land flowing with milk and honey, and will give it to us. Only do not rebel against the Lord. And do not be afraid of the people of the land, because we will swallow them up. Their protection is gone, but the Lord is with us. Do not be afraid of them." (Numbers 14:5–9)*

Notice what Moses and Aaron did. They fell on their faces right there in front of the people. They didn't threaten the ten spies, and they didn't plead with the people. They simply cast themselves on the mercy of God.

Notice what Joshua and Caleb did. They tore their clothes in grief, stood boldly before God and the agitated Israelites, and pled with them to trust God. No matter how big the people were—no matter how fortified their cities seemed to be—God was bigger; God was stronger.

Don't ever forget: when order becomes chaos, spiritual warfare has erupted in your life. If trust is broken, and the rumor mill cranks up, don't rely on your own strength to battle against the forces that hinder your progress. Trust only in the power and might of God. It is God who can quell the fight. It is God who can re-establish trust. It is God who will allow truth to triumph.

When Moses, Aaron, Joshua, and Caleb humbled themselves, when they grieved over the sin of their people, and when Joshua and Caleb stood boldly beside their leaders, God responded. Just as the Israelites were talking about stoning Moses and Aaron, the glory of the Lord (in the form of a cloud) appeared at the Tent of Meeting and all the Israelites saw Him. This is where Moses applied David's keys. Moses prayed and asked God to do what only He can do amid this desperate situation: "The Lord said to Moses, 'How long will these people treat me with contempt? How long will they refuse to believe in me, in spite of all the miraculous signs I have performed among them? I will strike them down with a plague and destroy them, but I will make you into a nation greater and stronger than they'" (Numbers 14:11–12).

God's patience was exhausted, and He was ready to drop back and punt. He'd done this before—remember Noah and the flood? What is it to God to be done with these "ignorant, stubborn" people and simply start again? He's got all the time in the world! He doesn't have to use them.

But Moses, through his love relationship with God, appealed to God on behalf of the nation that stood ready to stone him. Only God could have placed that kind of love in Moses' heart. Any ordinary man would have jumped at the chance for that kind of greatness. Notice how Moses prayed through each of David's keys.

Key 1:
Base Your Appeal to God on Your Relationship with Him

Moses said to the Lord, "Then the Egyptians will hear about it! By your power you brought these people up from among them. And they will tell the inhabitants of this land about it. They have already heard that you, O Lord, are with these people and that you, O Lord, have been seen face to face, that your cloud stays over them, and that you go before them in a pillar of cloud by day and a pillar of fire by night. If you put these people to death all at one time, the nations who have heard this report about you will say, 'The Lord was not able to bring these people into the land he promised them on oath; so he slaughtered them in the desert.'" (Numbers 14:13–16)

Basically Moses said, "These are Your people, oh God. Your name is attached to them. The rest of the world is talking about how Your people are different because they are Yours.

What will people say if You kill them here? What will they say about You?" Moses based his appeal on Israel's relationship with God.

Key 2:
Base Your Appeal to God
on His Righteousness and Not Your Own

Moses continued interceding for the Israelites using this second key: "In accordance with your great love, forgive the sin of these people, just as you have pardoned them from the time they left Egypt until now" (Numbers 14:19).

Notice that not once did Moses say anything about the righteousness of the people. He appealed to God's great love and compassion. Moses reminded God of what He'd done over and over again for these people. Moses simply asked God to forgive them again, as He'd done so many times before. Moses asked God to increase the greatness of His loving-kindness by extending forgiveness again.

What a powerful way to pray for people who have strayed from the Lord! Lay off the listing of their attributes, or their giftedness or merit. Veer away from whining to God about how their sin is hurting you, and instead acknowledge their desperate need for forgiveness and your confidence in God's compassion.

Key 3:
Face and State the Reality of the Situation

"If you put these people to death all at one time, the nations who have heard this report about you will say, 'The Lord was not able to bring these people into the land he promised them on oath; so he slaughtered them in the desert.'" (Numbers 14:15–16)

Moses spoke candidly with God, "OK, if that is what You will do, this is what's going to happen." Notice how bold Moses was before God. Moses' boldness did not come from a lack of reverence. It came from an intimate personal relationship. His boldness was fueled by His willingness to partner with God in leading these people. Moses allowed God to place His love for the people in Moses' heart. That love compelled Moses to boldly intercede for them even when they wanted to stone him and God was angry.

Key 4:
Base Your Appeal to God
on the Ways He's Worked in the Past

Moses said to the Lord, "Then the Egyptians will hear about it! By your power you brought these people up from among them. And they will tell the inhabitants of this land about it. They have already heard that you, O Lord, are with these people and that you, O Lord, have been seen face to face, that your cloud stays over them, and that you go before them

in a pillar of cloud by day and a pillar of fire by night. If you put these people to death all at one time, the nations who have heard this report about you will say, 'The Lord was not able to bring these people into the land he promised them on oath; so he slaughtered them in the desert.' . . . In accordance with your great love, forgive the sin of these people, just as you have pardoned them from the time they left Egypt until now." (Numbers 14:13–16, 19)

Moses reminded God of all that He had done for Israel ever since the days of Egypt. Then he made the point that God does not give to His children because they are deserving of His kindness. *God gives to us because He is God, and giving is His nature.* Sometimes we act as if we deserve God's blessings—may it never be! Let us rather learn to trust His mercy and grace, acknowledging that we have *nothing* to offer in return.

Key 5:
Base Your Appeal to God
on His Character

Although I've already quoted the following part of Moses' prayer, I repeat it here because it includes his appeal to the character of God: "Now may the Lord's strength be displayed, just as you have declared: 'The Lord is slow to anger, abounding in love and forgiving sin and rebellion. Yet he does not leave the guilty unpunished; he punishes the children for the sin of the fathers to the third and fourth generation.' In accordance with your great love, forgive the sin of these people, just as you have pardoned them from the time they left Egypt until now" (Numbers 14:17–18).

Remember how God revealed His character to Moses? Here's the exact moment for which that revelation was made. Moses asked for mercy for the people of Israel by reminding God of what He said about Himself. Moses was basically saying, "If You will spare Your people now, You will act according to who You are! You said yourself that You are slow to anger and abundant in lovingkindness, forgiving iniquity and transgression. If there were ever a time to be this way, now is it! Please, forgive these people!"

Do you want to know how God responded to Moses' prayer? Read Numbers 14:20–45. God spared the nation just as Moses asked Him to. But He sent them back to wander in the desert another forty years. The ten disobedient spies died of a plague; only Joshua and Caleb survived. The children of these Israelites (the ones who they worried would be taken as plunder) grew up to become the army that Joshua led. Those children served in the army that experienced God's supernatural victory when they chose to place their confidence in Him.

Oh God, Please . . .

Discussion Questions

1. Which part of Moses' prayer surprised you?

2. How might you take this prayer and apply it to your circumstance?

Pray: *Father, may we follow the example of Moses and apply David's keys to our often-locked hearts. Thank You, Lord. Thank You that goodness is Your nature. Thank You that You are the Lord, the compassionate and gracious God, slow to anger, abounding in love and faithfulness, maintaining love to thousands, and forgiving wickedness, rebellion, and sin. Oh God, may Your Presence go with us and give us rest.*

PART 4

❦

When You Doubt God

Faith is to believe what we do not see,
and the reward of this faith is
to see what we believe.

—

ST. AUGUSTINE

CHAPTER 23

When You Doubt God's Power

You are awesome, O God, in your sanctuary; the God of Israel gives power and strength to his people.

— PSALM 68:35

It's time to take your doubts into account. Don't let them flit about heckling you. Take each one by the tail and examine it. You chose to read this book because you wanted to learn how to overcome doubt. As I've shared my heart and my thoughts with you, I've imagined the source of your doubt. I am making the assumption that my doubts rise up from the same breeding grounds. Doubt plagues me when I pray because I don't "hear" God's voice. So, I dedicated the first eleven chapters of this book to hearing God when He speaks and learning how to deal effectively with His silence. I know, beyond a shadow of a doubt, that when you apply the five keys to your prayer life you will delete doubt from your prayers. But it might take time to develop the daily practice of exercising those keys to prayer. I hope that you saw the difference between what happened to the Israelites, who doubted God, and Joshua and Caleb, who chose to believe.

In these final chapters of this book, we will examine each doubt one at a time. As you take the time to define then dissect and finally defeat each doubt, you will have practical tools for addressing each of these doubts as often as they decide to torment you. Let's get started.

Define Your Doubt

To doubt God's power is to face an impossible situation or a crisis and decide that you are in big trouble because God is not able to bring you through. This doubt proclaims: God is not able! Here are three biblical examples of people who doubted God's power.

Example 1: The children of Israel when they were waiting to enter the Promised Land. We just talked about them. When their spies saw the size of Canaan's people and the fortifications of Canaan's cities, they decided that the power of their enemy was greater than the power of God (Numbers 13–14).

Example 2: The Israelite army that was assembled in the Valley of Elah. The moment the Philistine champion named Goliath marched toward the battle line, the Israelites determined that the Philistine giant was bigger than their God (1 Samuel 17).

Example 3: The night Jesus' disciples were caught in a storm. Even though Jesus was in the boat with them, the waves were so "furious" that His disciples feared for their lives. They decided that the furious squall was more powerful than God (Mark 4:35–41).

Dissect Your Doubt

I happen to be married to a very logically minded man, and we have a very logically minded daughter. Both of them use reason with their faith. Often they proclaim that to *not* believe just doesn't make sense. Let's use the sense of reason to dissect this doubt.

Consider the Creative Power of God

Genesis 1 gives us an account of the creative power of God: "In the beginning God created the heavens and the earth" (Genesis 1:1). As we read the creation story, we discover that God merely spoke the world into order: "And God said, 'Let there be light,' and there was light. . . . And God said, 'Let there be an expanse between the waters to separate water from water. . . . And it was so" (vv. 3, 6–7).

And God said, . . . And it was so.

And so continues the account of the creation of the world. God spoke the world into order, then He took a handful of dirt and formed it into man. That is the creative power of God.

Consider the Conquering Power of God

Before the Israelites ever camped on the edge of the Promised Land, they had already experienced the conquering power of God. Through a series of supernatural events, God brought down the world's super power of that day: Egypt. God used gnats and frogs, hail and locusts, and even a "death angel" to demonstrate His conquering power. It's hard for me to imagine how the Israelites could be so quick to doubt. But then again, I realize that I often succumb to doubt when faced with giants although God has performed the impossible in my life too.

Consider the conquering power of God in the face of the Philistine's warrior. Because Goliath was bigger, stronger, and more fierce and powerful than any of Israel's soldiers, God chose to use a shepherd boy to remind them that they didn't fight their enemy in their own strength. David faced Goliath and told everyone within the sound of his voice that he wasn't about to take Goliath down. To demonstrate His power, God was about to use David to kill that giant. David claimed the conquering power of God when he stood face to face with an impossible situation (see 1 Samuel 17:46–47).

Consider the Authoritative Power of God

I love this power the most. Often Scripture tells us that God is the ultimate authority. He answers only to Himself. And whatever God has said He will do, He is bound by His own holiness to fulfill His word. If we would meditate on this truth and it only, we would dispel most all our other doubts. "For no matter how many promises God has made, they are 'Yes' in Christ. And so through him the 'Amen' is spoken by us to the glory of God" (2 Corinthians 1:20). "God is not a man, that he should lie, nor a son of man, that he should change his mind. Does he speak and then not act? Does he promise and not fulfill?" (Numbers 23:19).

When Jesus' disciples got into the boat, Jesus said, "Let us go to the other side." They should have known then that if Jesus told them

> Lord, what joy to know that Your powers are so much greater than those of the enemy.
>
> CORRIE TEN BOOM

they were going to the other side, no storm in all of creation could stop them from getting there. But instead, Jesus' disciples doubted His power to do what He said He would do. If they'd known God better, they would have known that it was absolutely impossible for God not to keep His word.

A few years ago Kaleigh (my logically minded daughter) was having trouble making sense out of something that was going on in our family's life. She struggled with the obvious consequences of decisions that had been made and their contrast with the promises I was claiming from God's Word. I will be quite frank with you and confess that I was having the same struggle. But in her quiet time she ran across Hebrews 11:19a: "Abraham *reasoned* that God could raise the dead." This was in reference to Abraham's act of obedience in offering his son

Isaac as a sacrifice to God. Abraham knew full well that Isaac was the son God had promised him, and he reasoned in his mind that if God expected him to sacrifice his son, then God would raise Isaac from the dead. For Abraham reasoned that it would be easier for God to raise Isaac from the dead than it would be for God to break His promise. That revelation was enough for Kaleigh to reason in her mind that although we didn't have a clue how God was going to keep the promises He'd made in His Word regarding our family crisis, somehow, someway God would work it out.

God is the ultimate authority. All other beings in heaven and on earth bow down to Him: "He is the image of the invisible God, the firstborn over all creation. For by him all things were created: things in heaven and on earth, visible and invisible, whether thrones or powers or rulers or authorities; all things were created by him and for him. He is before all things, and in him all things hold together. And he is the head of the body, the church; he is the beginning and the firstborn from among the dead, so that in everything he might have the supremacy" (Colossians 1:15–18).

Defeat Your Doubt

Consider your particular situation, and ask yourself these questions:

→ Do I need God to demonstrate more power than what it took for Him to speak the world into existence?

→ Is this bigger than Goliath?

→ If God holds all things together, can He take care of this too?

As you consider the answer to each of those questions, talk to God about your convictions concerning His power.

Oh God, Please . . .

Discussion Questions

1. Why do you often doubt God's power?

2. What are some indications of God's creative power that you most appreciate in nature?

3. When have you experienced a demonstration of God's conquering power?

4. How does knowing that God has authoritative power impact the way that you pray?

Pray: *Oh God, when I get still and quiet, I realize that You are powerful. How could I ever doubt that You have power to take care of* [whatever your need is now]? *I look at the sunset and am reminded that You paint an original masterpiece every single day. I hear the birds and marvel at the mystery of their songs. I walk on the beach and am amazed that somehow you knit the tide with the moon and tilted the earth just right. I recognize that You hold all things in order, and if You can hold the whole world in the palm of Your hand, You can certainly* [do whatever You need Him to do for you].

CHAPTER 24

When You Doubt God's Concern

Those who know your name will trust in you, for you, Lord, have never forsaken those who seek you.

— PSALM 9:10

Define Your Doubt

This might be one of the most ferocious doubts that we face. Few of us can deny God's power; we see it demonstrated in nature every single day. But while we believe that God *can* provide solutions to our life's problems, we often doubt that He will. The doubt that God will answer us when we pray is rooted in a deep-seated belief that He might be concerned about much bigger things and just not that particularly concerned about us. This doubt might also be "watered" with experiences in our past when we feel as if God let us down.

The fertile ground for doubting God's personal interest is plowed up by a serious misunderstanding of God. When we doubt God's concern, we doubt God cares.

> To doubt God's care is to fall short of the abundant life that God has promised you.

Let's look again at one of the examples we considered in the last chapter. When the Israelites were perched on the edge of the Promised Land, they doubted God's power; they then determined that because God was not able He apparently didn't care. First the spies proclaimed, "'We can't attack those people; they are stronger than we are.' And they spread among the Israelites a bad report about the land they had explored" (Numbers 13:31–32).

Then, the Israelites allowed their first doubt in God's power to conceive and give birth to their second one: "If only we had died in Egypt! Or in this desert! Why is the Lord bringing us to this land only to let us fall by the sword? Our wives and children will be taken as plunder. Wouldn't it be better for us to go back to Egypt?" (Numbers 14:2–3).

Doubting God's care offends Him. Read His response to their doubt: "Nevertheless, as surely as I live and as surely as the glory of the Lord fills the whole earth, not one of the men who saw my glory and the miraculous signs I performed in Egypt and in the desert but who disobeyed me and tested me ten times—not one of them will ever see the land I promised on oath to their forefathers. No one who has treated me with contempt will ever see it" (Numbers 14:21–23).

Don't miss this truth: your doubt will not only keep you from experiencing God's power in your life but it will also pave the way for you to suffer terrible consequences. While the Israelite nation went on to live in the land God promised them, these particular Israelites died in the desert. They never experienced the fulfillment of God's promise in their lives. To doubt God's care is to fall short of the abundant life that God has promised you.

Dissect Your Doubt

Using our reasoning skills and God's Word, let's examine this doubt: Does God care?

When I read the Israelites' complaint in Numbers 14:2–4, I want to shout out loud, "Of course God cares! If He'd destined you for death and your children for plunder, why would He have gone to the trouble of rescuing you from your taskmasters in Egypt?" Their reasoning is absurd.

Doubt is often generated by fear. Fear fuels doubt. Of course, doubt also fuels fear. The two go together. But when fear gets out of hand, it's like a grass fire. My brother-in-law is a park ranger in Florida. One of his responsibilities is to train the volunteers who help to extinguish the grass fires that run rampant in dry seasons. These grass fires can quickly get out of control. Fear is like that. When doubt ignites fear, fear consumes faith. If fear is left to burn, our faith decreases, our doubts increase, and before long even our reasoning becomes absurd.

Anyone with a sound mind knows that the Israelites were not making any sense at all. The God who freed them from slavery, the same One who took the time to guide them through the wilderness and give them instructions for life, the God who fed them and gave them victory in battle would certainly *not* desert them now. For Him to do so would not make any sense at all.

Defeat Your Doubt

The only way I can figure that the Israelites were given over to such absurd thinking is that they didn't know God personally. Evidently they didn't understand how much they meant to Him. The only way to defeat this particular doubt is to truly understand how much God loves you. Anytime you are tempted to ask a question that begins with "Why would God . . ." you can know that you are dealing with this particular doubt.

Here are some facts from God's Word that you can use to defeat this doubt: "But God demonstrates his own love for us in this: While we were still sinners, Christ died for us" (Romans 5:8). If God was willing to give His very own Son to redeem your life from eternal separation from Him, you know that He cares for you.

Try doing this: plug the words *how much more* into the search engine of any Bible background website and see all the references to *how much more* God loves you. Here are a few:

> *If that is how God clothes the grass . . . will he not much more clothe you, O you of little faith? (Matthew 6:30)*

> *If you, then, though you are evil, know how to give good gifts to your children, how much more will your Father in heaven give good gifts to those who ask him! (Matthew 7:11)*

> *How much more valuable is a man than a sheep! (Matthew 12:12)*

> *Consider the ravens: They do not sow or reap, they have no storeroom or barn; yet God feeds them. And how much more valuable you are than birds! (Luke 12:24)*

God cares for you. He gave His very own Son to die for you, and *how much more* can anyone do than that? When you are tempted to doubt God's care, cling to these truths. Once you decide that God does care, you can stop asking absurd questions and start looking for how God is waiting for you to demonstrate great faith in the midst of confusing situations.

Oh God, Please . . .

Discussion Questions

1. When is the last time you doubted God's care? What questions did you ask?

2. How might the Israelite's faith have impacted their lives?

3. Why does God consider doubt "contempt"? How does it make you feel to realize that your actions and attitudes can be offensive to God?

Pray: *Lord, I confess that I doubt Your care at times. I realize that by doing so I offend You. After all You gave Your own Son to die for me! What greater love is there than that? Lord, please forgive me for letting the circumstances overwhelm me. Help me to anchor my thoughts on the solid surface of truth and to embrace the fact that Your Word is truth (John 17:17). I commit myself to reading Your Word daily so that I will be filling my mind with truth. Then the next time I am faced with the opportunity to exercise my faith, I will be ready.*

CHAPTER 25

When You Doubt God's Wisdom

Trust in the Lord with all your heart and lean not on your own understanding; in all your ways acknowledge him, and he will make your paths straight.

— PROVERBS 3:5-6

When my daughter Mikel turned eighteen, I invited about eighteen women together to celebrate her birthday. These were women who'd poured into her life either through Sunday school or through prayer partnerships or sports. Each woman brought Mikel a Bible verse and a word of wisdom to help guide her into the adult world. As the women shared their verses, we began to laugh, for almost every woman who'd gathered to bless Mikel on her eighteenth birthday chose Proverbs 3:5–6 as their verse to share. We realized that God had a word for Mikel, and Proverbs 3:5–6 was it.

These verses encourage us to trust God not with our heads but with our hearts. When you doubt God's wisdom, you determine to go your own way instead of His. At some point you decide that you know better than God how to direct your life.

Define Your Doubt

Perhaps the best way to define this doubt is to begin with defining *wisdom*. Wisdom is the ability to discern or judge what is true, right, or lasting.[7] So to doubt God's wisdom is to assume that He is not cable of discerning what is true, right, and lasting. While that might sound ridiculous, when you doubt God's wisdom you are most likely doubting that He knows better than you what is true, right, or lasting for you.

Perhaps this is rebellion against God's authority in your life rather than doubt. Who can profess Jesus as Savior and Lord and then turn around and harbor misgivings over His ability to know what is best? Who has more wisdom than God?

A great biblical example of doubting God's wisdom is found in the story of Jonah. The word of the Lord came to Jonah and told him to go to Nineveh and "preach against it." Most of us are so familiar with this story that we shake our heads knowingly at Jonah's foolishness. But, think about his assignment. Nineveh was wicked, it was quite a large city, and Jonah's message was to confront the Ninevites in their wickedness! Who wants to do that? We don't even want to confront our children in their sin much less point out the sin of strangers!

So, you know what Jonah did? He doubted the wisdom of God. Jonah decided that it would be better not to go to Nineveh—to go to Tarshish instead. Tarshish was in the opposite direction of Nineveh. In other words, Jonah heard God's instructions, doubted the wisdom of them, and fled from God. The story goes on, and we learn that we can run but we can't hide from

> God doesn't define truth—He is truth.

God. But once Jonah found himself in the belly of a big fish, he came to grips with the foolishness of doubting God's wisdom. Jonah prayed a powerful prayer of confession praising God for His salvation. And once the fish expelled Jonah, he "obeyed the word of the Lord and went to Nineveh" (see Jonah 1–2 and Jonah 3:3).

Dissect Your Doubt

When you find yourself doubting God's wisdom, consider these things.

God has been around a whole lot longer than you; He was there in the beginning and He will be there in the end. Who has a better perspective on life than God?

Not only has God been around forever, and not only will He be around forever, He also embodies truth and righteousness. God doesn't define truth—He is truth. Throughout God's Word His righteousness and truth are demonstrated through His acts of kindness, goodness, compassion, power, and love. Who but God offers us a better understanding of what is true, right, and lasting?

Don't forget that you have a nemesis, and his name is Satan. Satan operates under clouds of deception. He taints truth and contaminates reality. He works in the shadows of darkness. He loves to challenge God's wisdom. His tactic is to focus your attention on your own wisdom and divert your attention from God's. Satan does this by distracting you from worship. Don't forget that God speaks through worship.

One of the reasons Jonah disobeyed God was his own prejudice. Jonah didn't like the people in Nineveh, and he didn't want to see them saved. Like many of us, Jonah was selfish. Oftentimes we doubt God's wisdom because we don't share His love for people. Our own selfish plans seem to make more sense to us.

To doubt God's wisdom is to disregard the nature of His infinity, to ignore his character, to pay no attention to the work of Satan, and to harbor prejudice and selfish desires.

Defeat Your Doubt

Perhaps the best way to defeat this doubt is with a good dose of surrender. When you surrender your limited experience, knowledge, and selfish desires to God, then you will overcome the temptation to doubt His wisdom.

Proverbs 20:29 declares that while the glory of young men is in their strength, the glory of old men is in their gray hair. The implication is that after living lots of life one has more wisdom. I've lived long enough to recognize this truth. Unfortunately many of the strong young men (and women) are not interested in learning from those with gray (or in my case, colored) hair. However, when it comes to defeating the temptation to doubt God's wisdom, consider Revelation 22:13. If longevity gives one wisdom, then God has the most: "I am the Alpha and the Omega, the First and the Last, the Beginning and the End."

The entire book of Proverbs exhorts the reader to choose God's wisdom. In doing so, you are choosing life. Proverbs 9:10 tells where wisdom begins: "The fear of the Lord is the beginning of wisdom, and knowledge of the Holy One is understanding." In defeating doubt there is no substitute for a reverent fear (and honor) of the Lord and a solid knowledge of His ways. The best way to establish fear, reverence, honor, and knowledge is to read the Bible daily and do what it says.

Finally, the best antidote to doubting God's wisdom is praise. When you get into the practice of declaring God's goodness, His faithfulness, love, compassion, forgiveness, knowledge, righteousness, justice, you are reminded consistently that there is no wisdom like God's.

Oh God, Please . . .

Discussion Questions

1. Do you agree with the statement "To doubt God's wisdom is to rebel against Him"? Why or why not?

2. Share about a time when praising God brought you out of a place of doubt.

3. Search the book of Proverbs for verses pertaining to wisdom. Share these verses.

Pray: *Lord, I do doubt Your wisdom at times. I cry out in agony over what seems to me to be madness. I have a hard time understanding how You will take the circumstances of my life and transform them into good. But when I consider that You are the First and the Last, the Beginning and the End, it seems ludicrous for me to entertain doubt. Who knows better than You how to bring glory to Yourself out of my surrendered life? That's it—isn't it, Lord? I need to surrender. I need to surrender my reasoning to Yours; I need to surrender my suffering for Your greater glory. I need to surrender what I don't know (which is plenty) to what You do know (which is everything). I proclaim right now that I believe You know what You're doing and You are much better at directing my life than I am.*

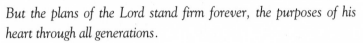

CHAPTER 26

When You Doubt God's Plan

But the plans of the Lord stand firm forever, the purposes of his heart through all generations.

— PSALM 33:11

To doubt God's plan is to make an initial commitment to follow His lead only to take over leadership midstream. Most people don't even know when they are suffering from this doubt. They just quit praying, perhaps stop attending church, and begin to make decisions without reading God's Word or asking for His input.

Other people know full well that they are diverting from God's plan. They come to a moment of decision and decide to do things their own way and step outside the protective boundaries He's set up for them in the Bible. For instance, many young people today decide to have sex and live with their significant others outside of marriage. Many of these same young people dedicated their lives to Christ as children in vacation Bible school or as teenagers at youth camp.

Define Your Doubt

Just like doubting God's wisdom, when you doubt God's plan you are dealing more with the issue of surrender than that of faith. Then again, perhaps, if you had enough faith you would find that complete surrender to God is the only thing that really makes sense.

I am not rebellious by nature, but I am selfish. When I accepted Jesus as my Savior, I understood that I was not only receiving His generous gift of eternal life but that I was also giving Him control over the life I live during the rest of my days on earth. I was eleven years old; this was not a commitment that was hard for me to make. The year after I accepted

Jesus as Lord I learned Jeremiah 29:11: "'For I know the plans I have for you,' declares the Lord, 'plans to prosper you and not to harm you, plans to give you hope and a future.'"

> If you doubt God's plan, you are dealing more with the issue of surrender than that of faith.

Those plans sounded good to me! I liked the prospects of prosperity. I didn't want to be harmed, and hope and a future sounded good too. Jeremiah 29:11 became my guiding light throughout my teenage years and on into college. Even in seminary when I was looking for a husband, I banked on Jeremiah 29:11. But when my husband Tom and I got to Thompson's Station, Tennessee, and I was ready to have children, I questioned God's plans. My questions went something like this,

- "Lord, You told me that Your plans were to prosper me and not to harm me, to give me a hope and a future. If that is so, why won't You let me become pregnant?"

- "Oh God, please! Let Your plan include children for Tom and me!"

- "Why wouldn't You include children in Your plans? If You never intended for me to be a mother, why did You plant such a desire in my heart?"

Because my life was not going the way I planned for it to go, I began to doubt God's plan.

Dissect Your Doubt

Perhaps I've stepped on your toes with some of the other doubts we've discussed. If it helps you to feel a bit better, know that I'm stepping on my own toes with this one. As often as my plans differ from God's, I have a tendency to doubt that His plans are better. Not only am I a pretty good planner, but I like to think that I am also in tune with what God wants for me and from me. Therefore, when my plans are disrupted, I worry about His ability to get His plans back on (my) track.

Let's dissect Jeremiah 29:11–14.

> *"For I know the plans I have for you," declares the Lord, "plans to prosper you and not to harm you, plans to give you hope and a future. Then you will call upon me and come and pray to me, and I will listen to you. You will seek me and find me when you seek me with all your heart. I will be found by you," declares the Lord, "and will bring you back from captivity. I will gather you from all the nations and places where I have banished you," declares the Lord "and will bring you back to the place from which I carried you in exile."*

According to Jeremiah 29:11, who knows the plans for your life? God!

What kind of plans does He have for you? His plans are to prosper you, to give you a hope and a future.

What will God do when you pray? According to verse 12, God will listen to you when you pray.

When will you find Him? You will find God when you seek Him with all your heart.

Once you are found, what will God do with you? Once you find Him, He will gather you from wherever you are and bring you back to live smack dab in the middle of His best for your life (I took a few liberties with this answer).

Jeremiah 29:11 is still my life verse. When I first read the words, my initial response was, "Great! God has a plan for me!" It was exciting to think that the Lord of all creation cared enough about me to have plans for my life. And for the longest time, I pursued that plan. But this is how I pursued it: My understanding was that God has a plan for MY life! A plan to prosper ME and not to harm ME, to give ME a hope and a future!

Can you see how I took the promise of Jeremiah 29:11 and placed ME in the middle of it? It took me several years and lots of life experiences to realize that was not at all what God had in mind when He revealed His plan to Jeremiah.

First of all, this verse was not written to me. It was written as a promise to the people of Israel—God's chosen people, His precious children, those who fulfilled His covenant relationship with Abraham. The original context of this passage is prophecy. To better understand these verses, we need to consider what was going on in Israel when Jeremiah first penned them.

Jeremiah fulfilled his ministry during the final forty years preceding Judah's fall into captivity to the Babylonians. Much of his book deals with that pending disaster. It also deals with God's desire for Israel to understand that the Babylonian take-over would be punishment for their rejection of the covenant they had with Him.

The specific responsibilities of Israel's covenant relationship with God are recorded in Deuteronomy 27 and 28. Deuteronomy 27:9 says, "Then Moses and the priests, who are Levites, said to all Israel, 'Be silent, O Israel, and listen! You have now become the people of the Lord your God. Obey the Lord your God and follow his commands and decrees that I give you today.'" Deuteronomy 28:1 says, "If you fully obey the Lord your God and carefully follow all his commands I give you today, the Lord your God will set you high above all nations on earth."

Then the verses that follow in Deuteronomy 28:2–14 describe the incredible blessings promised the Israelites as a result of their choosing to live within the boundaries (limits) set by their call (to be the people of God). Following the list of the blessings is a serious warning. Deuteronomy 28:15 says, "However, if you do not obey the Lord your God and do not carefully follow all his commands and decrees I am giving you today, all these curses will come upon you and overtake you."

After Moses warned the Israelites of the consequences of their disobedience, he then went into considerable detail regarding the various ways these curses would be executed against them in Deuteronomy 28:16–68. One particularly interesting verse is 49: "The Lord will bring a nation against you from far away, from the ends of the earth, like an eagle swooping down, a nation whose language you will not understand."

This verse points to the moment in time that Jeremiah was called to be a prophet. Much of his book is written to Israel to explain why she is about to be punished and what all that punishment would entail. However, God did not want His people to think they'd been abandoned (even though they had already abandoned Him). So, He allowed Jeremiah a glimpse into what was to come after their Babylonian captivity. Jeremiah 29:10 puts the promise of verses 11–14 in historical context: "This is what the Lord says: 'When seventy years are completed for Babylon, I will come to you and fulfill my gracious promise to bring you back to this place.'"

After the inevitable punishment Israel received for her sins, she once again experienced redemption. And that begins the promise of Jeremiah 29:11.

> You were created to be loved by God and to fulfill the work He prepared for you to do.

So, you might ask me, "What does all this background information have to do with the application of that promise to my life today?" I'm glad you asked. Although this verse was not written specifically to you, the God who promised is the same One you serve today. And when you put yourself in the middle of the passage, the working of His love will extend to you just as it extended to Israel when Jeremiah wept.

- ✦ God has plans for you. Ephesians 2:10 reinforces this truth: "For we are God's workmanship, created in Christ Jesus to do good works, which God prepared in advance for us to do."
- ✦ Those plans *are* to prosper you, to give you a hope and a future. Romans 8:28 tells you that even when circumstances seem to rob you of the prosperity and hope, God assures you He is still on His throne, and His plans remain for your good: "And we know that in all things God works for the good of those who love him, who have been called according to his purpose."
- ✦ But here's the important thing: they are God's plans and not your own!

Defeat Your Doubt

The plans God has for you are for your good and His glory! They are plans that impact His larger plan. We are on this earth for only a fraction of time—we take up only a fraction of space. God has a great big plan unfolding that began "In the beginning" and will conclude with "Amen." He rules the universe, and in His good pleasure He chose to create you. You were created to be loved by God and to fulfill the work He prepared in advance for you to do. Only when you acknowledge Him as Lord and choose to live within the boundaries of your relationship with Him will you fully embrace the truth of Jeremiah 29:11.

By submitting to God's higher purposes and greater plans, you will defeat the doubt that challenges God's right to plan your life.

Oh God, Please . . .

Discussion Questions

1. How does knowing that God has plans for your life help you define the boundaries He has set for you?

2. What does God's prosperity look like?

3. What future does God have waiting for you?

Jeremiah's life of prosperity and hope: Don't you find it ironic that the verse many of us cling to as a guarantee for a life without suffering or pain was penned by the man they called "the weeping prophet"? When Jeremiah accepted his call to ministry (which included the surrender of wife and children, popularity and worldly success), he was used by God to forewarn God's people of their coming judgment (the fulfillment of the curse set before them in Deuteronomy 28). The message he bore was so full of sorrow that Jeremiah wept (Jeremiah 9:1), and most scholars believe this "weeping prophet" also wrote Lamentations (another book in the Old Testament that laments the destruction of Jerusalem at the hands of the Babylonians).

I say all that to remind you that this promise in Jeremiah 29:11 goes far beyond the earthly understanding of prosperity. The promise of Jeremiah 29:11 is anchored in the future that is ours through the life, death, and resurrection of Christ.

Pray: *Lord, thank You for telling me that as often as I pray, You hear me. I want to seek You with my whole heart. Show me where my heart is divided and what affections are in my heart that stand in opposition to Your purposes and Your plans. I want to fulfill the good work You prepared beforehand for me to do. I trust Your better plans for my life. Please reveal them to me.*

> *"'For I know the plans I have for you,'*
> *declares the Lord . . ."*
> JEREMIAH 29:11

CHAPTER 27

When You Doubt God's Love

I have loved you with an everlasting love; I have drawn you with loving-kindness.

— JEREMIAH 31:3

I asked two of my children how anyone could doubt God's love, and they both responded quickly. One said, "Well, if your dad died of a heart attack and then you found out that your husband had been having affairs throughout your entire marriage, and all of this happened in a matter of three months, you might doubt God's love." The other one said, "If you are in a car wreck and every member of your family dies except for you, you might doubt God's love."

There certainly are circumstances in life that can cause you to doubt God's love. What do you do when these circumstances are overwhelming?

Define Your Doubt

To doubt God's love is to be faced with such terrible tragedy that you cannot reconcile God's love with the pain, suffering, and loss you've experienced. To doubt God's love is to be swallowed up in grief and confusion. Some people point to the suffering in the world as an excuse for not having a personal relationship with God. They ask, "How can a God of love allow children to die of starvation and people to be tortured?"

When you doubt God's love, you live in frustration. If you have any relationship with God at all, you struggle with the God of Scripture and many of Scripture's promises and the God who hovers silently over your present condition. This is perhaps the most prevalent of all doubts.

Dissect Your Doubt

Remember those Israelites on the border of the Promised Land? They boarded a train of thought and went down the wrong track. When you choose to doubt God's love, you tend to board that train with them. Think about it.

Take the woman whose father died and whose husband had multiple affairs. Was her father's death God's fault? Were her husband's affairs somehow God's responsibility? Sure, God could've intervened and spared her father's life, but should we expect that of Him? To experience such heinous loss and then turn your focus heavenward and shake your earthly fist at God is to make God the defendant in a case where He is no more at fault than you are.

Do we expect God to let us define love and then hold Him to our definition? One writer quotes C. S. Lewis from his book *The Problem of Pain:*

> The problem of reconciling human suffering with the existence of a God who loves is only insoluble so long as we attach a trivial meaning to the word "love" and look on things as if man were the centre of them. Man is not the centre. God does not exist for the sake of man.

> Man does not exist for his own sake. "Thou hast created all things, and for thy pleasure they are and were created." We were made not primarily that we may love God (though we were made for that too) but that God may love us, that we may become objects in which the divine love may rest "well pleased."[8]

In order to come to grips with God's definition of love, you must come to grips with God. In 1 John 4:8 we learn that "God is love." God doesn't merely tell us how to love, nor does He only communicate love; God simply *IS* love.

God's love is demonstrated, exposed, and poured out on Calvary's cross. Because God loves us, for no other reason than that, He sent His own Son to deliver us from suffering and death. God is creating a new heaven and a new earth where there will be no more pain, suffering, or death (see Revelation 21:4). And until we get there, God Himself walks with us through pain and suffering. And if we will trust Him, He will see to it that every ounce of pain is woven together in a tapestry, in a masterpiece of love (see Romans 8:28).

Defeat Your Doubt

The best way to defeat your doubt about God's love is to confess that you will never have a complete understanding of God—neither will you ever understand the suffering that comes your way in this life. A few years ago I was asked to speak at the memorial service of a newborn baby boy. His mom and dad were members of our church, and after many years of infertility they became pregnant with this child. There is a whole lot more to

the story, but I will wrap it up to say that after several months of fervent prayer, this little baby died just as the doctors predicted he would. His mother called me and said, "Leighann, I know a lot of people have been praying for my baby, and they will be asking what his death has to do with prayer. Will you please address this at his memorial service?"

I am not ashamed to tell you that I responded to her request like this: "Melissa, I am one of those people who are desperately trying to reconcile all this! I am having trouble with it myself, but I would be honored to speak at your son's memorial service."

It was the hardest assignment I've ever had. When I got up to speak, I looked at the crowd of

> God's love is demonstrated, exposed, and poured out on Calvary's cross.

friends and family who were gathered and settled my gaze on Melissa and David, the baby's parents. Then, I shared that I'd been reading Isaiah 40 in my quiet time when Tom called to tell me that Elisha had been born and had then died. I shared some of the questions Isaiah asked in chapter 40 and told the congregation that a measure of comfort comes from recognizing the fact that although we serve a kind, good, and loving God, no matter how long we serve Him or how much time we spend with Him, He will continue to be beyond our understanding. I closed my message with an excerpt from C. S. Lewis's book *The Lion, the Witch and the Wardrobe* where the children are hearing for the first time of Aslan the Lion, the allegorical Christ figure of the book:

> "Ooh!" said Susan, "I'd thought he was a man. Is he—quite safe? I shall feel rather nervous about meeting a lion."

"That you will, dearie, and no mistake," said Mrs. Beaver, "if there's anyone who can appear before Aslan without their knees knocking, they're either braver than most or else silly."

"Then he isn't safe?" said Lucy.

"Safe?" said Mr. Beaver. "Don't you hear what Mrs. Beaver tells you? Who said anything about safe? 'Course he isn't safe. But he's good. He's the King, I tell you."[9]

He's the King. You won't always understand His ways. Sometimes horrible, terrible, devastating things will happen. Those things might leave you writhing in pain, but you do not suffer as those who have no hope (1 Thessalonians 4:13). If you turn to God in the midst of your suffering, He will come right down into the middle of the mess and take on the heavy load of your grief. You will not only make it through the valley of the shadow of death but you will come out on the other side with the incredible experience of having been with God in an intimate place.

At the end of my message at that baby boy's memorial service, I urged my friends to cling to what they do know when they were tempted to doubt God's love. And then we sang this song,

Jesus loves me, **this I know** . . .

Oh God, Please . . .

Discussion Questions

1. Have you ever doubted God's love? What caused you to doubt?

2. What Scriptures do you cling to when you wonder about God's love?

3. What would you say to the young woman who lost both her husband and her father within a matter of weeks? What would you say to the young boy whose family was killed in a car accident?

4. How do you know God's love?

Pray: *Oh God, if ever there were a reason to doubt Your love it would be when terribly bad things happen. We get confused because we are hurt. We are limited in our ability to see things from Your perspective, and mostly we need reassurance that You are near. Thank You for promising us that You are a very present help in time of trouble (Psalm 46:1). I choose to trust You. I choose to keep my eyes focused on the cross where Your love poured out. And I choose to hold tight to You until that day when I can see You clearly face to face.*

Appendix

APPENDIX 1

Scripture Used in This Book

When you are sick, you go to the doctor and she prescribes medicine that combats your illness. Just as a good antibiotic heals your physical body, so God's Word heals your spiritual body. To doubt is to allow spiritual sickness to run rampant through your system.

I've put a whole lot of Scripture in this book. Use this list as a tool—a quick, take a pill now! Print a verse on an index card and tuck it in your wallet. Type it into your personal device and read it throughout the day. Just as amoxicillin goes to work in your body, so God's Word will go to work in your mind and your heart to remove your doubt.

Scripture included in this book by chapter:

Introduction

Surely the arm of the Lord is not too short to save, nor his ear too dull to hear.

ISAIAH 59:1

Chapter 1

My God, my God, why have you forsaken me? Why are you so far from saving me, so far from the words of my groaning?

PSALM 22:1–2

I have much to say in judgment of you. But he who sent me is reliable, and what I have heard from him I tell the world.

JOHN 8:26

He who belongs to God hears what God says. The reason you do not hear is that you do not belong to God.

JOHN 8:47

Chapter 2

Your word is a lamp to my feet and a light for my path.

PSALM 119:105

"For I know the plans I have for you," declares the Lord, "plans to prosper you and not to harm you, plans to give you hope and a future."

JEREMIAH 29:11

Do you not know? Have you not heard? The Lord is the everlasting God, the Creator of the ends of the earth. He will not grow tired or weary, and his understanding no one can fathom. He gives strength to the weary and increases the power of the weak. Even youths grow tired and weary, and young men stumble and fall; but those who hope in the Lord will renew their strength. They will soar on wings like eagles; they will run and not grow weary, they will walk and not be faint.

ISAIAH 40:28–31

And my God will meet all your needs according to his glorious riches in Christ Jesus.

PHILIPPIANS 4:19

Chapter 3

But encourage one another daily, as long as it is called Today, so that none of you may be hardened by sin's deceitfulness.

HEBREWS 3:13

Chapter 4

"In the last days," God says, "I will pour out my Spirit on all people. Your sons and daughters will prophesy, your young men will see visions, your old men will dream dreams."

ACTS 2:17

Chapter 5

But thou art holy, O thou that inhabitest the praises of Israel.

PSALM 22:3 KJV

After consulting the people, Jehoshaphat appointed men to sing to the Lord and to praise him for the splendor of his holiness as they went out at the head of the army, saying: "Give thanks to the Lord, for his love endures forever."

2 CHRONICLES 20:21

Chapter 6

I am the good shepherd; I know my sheep and my sheep know me.

JOHN 10:14

I am the good shepherd. The good shepherd lays down his life for the sheep.

JOHN 10:11

Chapter 7

By their fruit you will recognize them. Do people pick grapes from thornbushes, or figs from thistles? Likewise every good tree bears good fruit, but a bad tree bears bad fruit.

MATTHEW 7:16–17

The man who enters by the gate is the shepherd of his sheep. The watchman opens the gate for him, and the sheep listen to his voice. He calls his own sheep by name and leads them out. When he has brought out all his own, he goes on ahead of them, and his sheep follow him because they know his voice. But they will never follow a stranger; in fact, they will run away from him because they do not recognize a stranger's voice.

JOHN 10:2–5

I am sending you out like lambs among wolves.

LUKE 10:3

Watch out for false prophets. They come to you in sheep's clothing, but inwardly they are ferocious wolves.

MATTHEW 7:15

Chapter 8

Oh my God, I cry out by day, but you do not answer, by night, and am not silent.

PSALM 22:2

Chapter 9

Oh Lord, hear my prayer, listen to my cry for mercy; in your faithfulness and righteousness come to my relief.

PSALM 143:1

Do not bring your servant into judgment, for no one living is righteous before you.

PSALM 143:2

Chapter 10

I spread out my hands to you; my soul thirsts for you like a parched land.

PSALM 143:6

Answer me quickly, O Lord; my spirit fails. Do not hide your face from me or I will be like those who go down to the pit. Let the morning bring me word of your unfailing love, for I have put my trust in you.

PSALM 143:7–8A

"'If you can?'" said Jesus. "Everything is possible for him who believes."

MARK 9:23

I do believe; help me overcome my unbelief!

MARK 9:24

Chapter 11

Teach me to do your will, for you are my God; may your good Spirit lead me on level ground.

PSALM 143:10

For your name's sake, O Lord, preserve my life; in your righteousness, bring me out of trouble. In your unfailing love, silence my enemies; destroy all my foes, for I am your servant.

PSALM 143:11–12

Chapter 12

In your unfailing love, silence my enemies; destroy all my foes, for I am your servant.

PSALM 143:12

Chapter 13

"There is not a righteous man on earth who does what is right and never sins."

ECCLESIASTES 7:20

"O Lord, hear my prayer, listen to my cry for mercy; in your faithfulness and righteousness come to my relief. Do not bring your servant into judgment, for no one living is righteous before you."

PSALM 143:1–2

"As it is written, 'There is no one righteous, not even one.'"

ROMANS 3:10

"For all of us have become like one who is unclean, and all our righteous deeds are like a filthy garment."

ISAIAH 64:6 NASB

Chapter 14

"Come now, and let us reason together," says the Lord. "Though your sins are like scarlet, they shall be as white as snow; though they are red as crimson, they shall be like wool."

ISAIAH 1:18

Do not bring your servant into judgment, for no one living is righteous before you.

PSALM 143:2

You see, at just the right time, when we were still powerless, Christ died for the ungodly. Very rarely will anyone die for a righteous man, though for a good man someone might possibly dare to die. But God demonstrates his own love for us in this: While we were still sinners, Christ died for us. Since we have now been justified by his blood, how much more shall we be saved from God's wrath through him! For if, when we were God's enemies, we were reconciled to him through the death of his Son, how much more, having been reconciled, shall we be saved through his life!

ROMANS 5:6–10

That if you confess with your mouth Jesus as Lord, and believe in your heart that God raised Him from the dead, you will be saved; for with the heart a person believes, resulting in righteousness, and with the mouth he confesses, resulting in salvation.

ROMANS 10:9–10 NASB

Chapter 15

For you have not received a spirit of slavery leading to fear again, but you have received a spirit of adoption as sons by which we cry out, "Abba! Father!" The Spirit Himself testifies with our spirit that we are children of God.

ROMANS 8:15–16 NASB

Therefore, there is now no condemnation for those who are in Christ Jesus, because through Christ Jesus the law of the Spirit of life set me free from the law of sin and death.

ROMANS 8:1–2

Those who live according to the sinful nature have their minds set on what that nature desires; but those who live in accordance with the Spirit have their minds set on what the Spirit desires.

ROMANS 8:5

You, however, are controlled not by the sinful nature but by the Spirit, if the Spirit of God lives in you. And if anyone does not have the Spirit of Christ, he does not belong to Christ.

ROMANS 8:9

Chapter 16

The enemy pursues me, he crushes me to the ground; he makes me dwell in darkness like those long dead. So my spirit grows faint within me; my heart within me is dismayed.

PSALM 143:3–4

The war between the house of Saul and the house of David lasted a long time. David grew stronger and stronger, while the house of Saul grew weaker and weaker.

2 SAMUEL 3:1

Chapter 17

Be self-controlled and alert. Your enemy the devil prowls around like a roaring lion looking for someone to devour. Resist him, standing firm in your faith, because you know that your brothers throughout the world are undergoing the same kind of sufferings.

1 PETER 5:8–9

When the woman saw that the fruit of the tree was good for food and pleasing to the eye, and also desirable for gaining wisdom, she took some and ate it. She also gave some to her husband, who was with her, and he ate it.

GENESIS 3:6

Chapter 18

I remember the days of long ago; I meditate on all your works and consider what your hands have done.

PSALM 143:5

You answer us with awesome deeds of righteousness, O God our Savior, the hope of all the ends of the earth and of the farthest seas, who formed the mountains by your power, having armed yourself with strength, who stilled the roaring of the seas, the roaring of their waves, and the turmoil of the nations.

Those living far away fear your wonders; where morning dawns and evening fades you call forth songs of joy. You care for the land and water it; you enrich it abundantly. The streams of God are filled with water to provide the people with grain, for so you have ordained it. You drench its furrows and level its ridges; you soften it with showers and bless its crops. You crown the year with your bounty, and your carts overflow with abundance. The grasslands of the desert overflow; the hills are clothed with gladness. The meadows are covered with flocks and the valleys are mantled with grain; they shout for joy and sing.

PSALM 65:5–13

Chapter 19

The Lord is gracious and compassionate, slow to anger and rich in love.

PSALM 145:8

Teach me to do your will, for you are my God; may your good Spirit lead me on level ground. For your name's sake, O Lord, preserve my life; in your righteousness, bring me out of trouble. In your unfailing love, silence my enemies; destroy all my foes, for I am your servant.

PSALM 143:10–12

Answer me quickly, O Lord; my spirit fails. Do not hide your face from me or I will be like those who go down to the pit. . . . For your name's sake, O Lord, preserve my life; in your righteousness, bring me out of trouble. In your unfailing love, silence my enemies; destroy all my foes, for I am your servant.

PSALM 143:7, 11–12

What, then, shall we say in response to this? If God is for us, who can be against us? He who did not spare his own Son, but gave him up for us all—how will he not also, along with him, graciously give us all things?

ROMANS 8:31–32

No, in all these things we are more than conquerors through him who loved us. For I am convinced that neither death nor life, neither angels nor demons, neither the present nor the future, nor any powers, neither height nor depth, nor anything else in all creation, will be able to separate us for the love of God that is in Christ Jesus our Lord.

ROMANS 8:37–39

Chapter 20

Then Caleb silenced the people before Moses and said, "We should go up and take possession of the land, for we can certainly do it."

NUMBERS 13:30

How will anyone know that you are pleased with me and with your people unless you go with us? What else will distinguish me and your people from all the other people on the face of the earth?

EXODUS 33:16

And he passed in front of Moses, proclaiming, "the Lord, the Lord, the compassionate and gracious God, slow to anger, abounding in love and faithfulness, maintaining love to thousands, and forgiving wickedness, rebellion and sin. Yet he does not leave the guilty unpunished; he punishes the children and their children for the sin of the fathers to the third and fourth generation."

EXODUS 34:6–7

Go up through the Negev and on into the hill country. See what the land is like and whether the people who live there are strong or weak, few or many. What kind of land do they live in? Is it good or bad? What kind of towns do they live in? Are they unwalled or fortified? How is the soil? Is it fertile or poor? Are there trees on it or not? Do your best to bring back some of the fruit of the land.

NUMBERS 13:17–20

Chapter 21

That night all the people of the community raised their voices and wept aloud.

NUMBERS 14:1

All the Israelites grumbled against Moses and Aaron, and the whole assembly said to them, "If only we had died in Egypt! Or in this desert! Why is the Lord bringing us to this land only to let us fall by the sword? Our wives and children will be taken as plunder. Wouldn't it be better for us to go back to Egypt?" And they said to each other, "We should choose a leader and go back to Egypt."

NUMBERS 14:2–4

Chapter 22

Moses said to the Lord, . . . "Now may the Lord's strength be displayed, just as you have declared."

NUMBERS 14:13, 17

Then Moses and Aaron fell facedown in front of the whole Israelite assembly gathered there. Joshua son of Nun and Caleb son of Jephunneh, who were among those who had explored the land, tore their clothes and said to the entire Israelite assembly, "The land we passed through and explored is exceedingly good. If the Lord is please with us, he will lead us into that land, a land flowing with milk and honey, and will give it to us. Only do not rebel against the Lord. And do not be afraid of the people of the land, because we will swallow them up. Their protection is gone, but the Lord is with us. Do not be afraid of them."

NUMBERS 14:5–9

The Lord said to Moses, "How long will these people treat me with contempt? How long will they refuse to believe in me, in spite of all the miraculous signs I have performed among them? I will strike them down with a plague and destroy them, but I will make you into a nation greater and stronger than they."

NUMBERS 14:11–12

Moses said to the Lord, "Then the Egyptians will hear about it! By your power you brought these people up from among them. And they will tell the inhabitants of this land about it. They have already heard that you, O Lord, are with these people and that you, O Lord, have been seen face to face, that your cloud stays over them, and that you go before them in a pillar of cloud by day and a pillar of fire by night. If you put these people to death all at one time, the nations who have heard this report about you will say, 'The Lord was not able to bring these people into the land he promised them on oath; so he slaughtered them in the desert.'"

NUMBERS 14:13–16

In accordance with your great love, forgive the sin of these people, just as you have pardoned them from the time they left Egypt until now.

NUMBERS 14:19

If you put these people to death all at one time, the nations who have heard this report about you will say, "The Lord was not able to bring these people into the land he promised them on oath; so he slaughtered them in the desert."

NUMBERS 14:15–16

Moses said to the Lord, "Then the Egyptians will hear about it! By your power you brought these people up from among them. And they will tell the inhabitants of this land about it. They have already heard that you, O Lord, are with these people and that you, O Lord, have been seen face to face, that your cloud stays over them, and that you go before them in a pillar of cloud by day and a pillar of fire by night. If you put these people to death all at one time, the nations who have heard this report about you will say, 'The Lord was not able to bring these people into the land he promised them on oath; so he slaughtered them in the desert.' . . . In accordance *with your great love, forgive the sin of these people, just as you have pardoned them from the time they left Egypt until now.*

NUMBERS 14:13–16, 19

Now may the Lord's strength be displayed, just as you have declared: "The Lord is slow to anger, abounding in love and forgiving sin and rebellion. Yet he does not leave the guilty unpunished; he punishes the children for the sin of the fathers to the third and fourth generation." In accordance with your great love, forgive the sin of these people, just as you have pardoned them from the time they left Egypt until now.

NUMBERS 14:17–18

Chapter 23

You are awesome, O God, in your sanctuary; the God of Israel gives power and strength to his people.

PSALM 68:35

In the beginning God created the heavens and the earth.

GENESIS 1:1

For no matter how many promises God has made, they are "Yes" in Christ. And so through him the "Amen" is spoken by us to the glory of God.

2 CORINTHIANS 1:20

God is not a man, that he should lie, nor a son of man, that he should change his mind. Does he speak and then not act? Does he promise and not fulfill?

NUMBERS 23:19

Abraham reasoned that God could raise the dead.

HEBREWS 11:19A

He is the image of the invisible God, the firstborn over all creation. For by him all things were created: things in heaven and on earth, visible and invisible, whether thrones or powers or rulers or authorities; all things were created by him and for him. He is before all things, and in him all things hold together. And he is the head of the body, the church; he is the beginning and the firstborn from among the dead, so that in everything he might have the supremacy.

COLOSSIANS 1:15–18

Chapter 24

Those who know your name will trust in you, for you, Lord, have never forsaken those who seek you.

PSALM 9:10

"We can't attack those people; they are stronger than we are." And they spread among the Israelites a bad report about the land they had explored.

NUMBERS 13:31–32

If only we had died in Egypt! Or in this desert! Why is the Lord bringing us to this land only to let us fall by the sword? Our wives and children will be taken as plunder. Wouldn't it be better for us to go back to Egypt?

NUMBERS 14:2–3

But God demonstrates his own love for us in this: While we were still sinners, Christ died for us.

ROMANS 5:8

Nevertheless, as surely as I live and as surely as the glory of the Lord fills the whole earth, not one of the men who saw my glory and the miraculous signs I performed in Egypt and in the desert but who disobeyed me and tested me ten times—not one of them will ever see the land I promised on oath to their forefathers. No one who has treated me with contempt will ever see it.

NUMBERS 14:21–23

If that is how God clothes the grass . . . will he not much more clothe you, O you of little faith?

MATTHEW 6:30

If you, then, though you are evil, know how to give good gifts to your children, how much more will your Father in heaven give good gifts to those who ask him!

MATTHEW 7:11

How much more valuable is a man than a sheep!

MATTHEW 12:12

Consider the ravens: They do not sow or reap, they have no storeroom or barn; yet God feeds them. And how much more valuable you are than birds!

LUKE 12:24

Chapter 25

Trust in the Lord with all your heart and lean not on your own understanding; in all your ways acknowledge him, and he will make your paths straight.

PROVERBS 3:5–6

The glory of young men is their strength, gray hair the splendor of the old.

PROVERBS 20:29

I am the Alpha and Omega, the First and the Last, the Beginning and the End.

REVELATION 22:13

The fear of the Lord is the beginning of wisdom, and knowledge of the Holy One is understanding.

PROVERBS 9:10

Chapter 26

But the plans of the Lord stand firm forever, the purposes of his heart through all generations.

PSALM 33:11

"For I know the plans I have for you," declares the Lord, "plans to prosper you and not to harm you, plans to give you hope and a future. Then you will call upon me and come and pray to me, and I will listen to you. You will seek me and find me when you seek me with all your heart. I will be found by you," declares the Lord, "and will bring you back from captivity. I will gather you from all the nations and places where I have banished you," declares the Lord "and will bring you back to the place from which I carried you in exile."

JEREMIAH 29:11–14

If you fully obey the Lord your God and carefully follow all his commands I give you today, the Lord your God will set you high above all nations on earth.

DEUTERONOMY 28:1

Then Moses and the priests, who are Levites, said to all Israel, "Be silent, O Israel, and listen! You have now become the people of the Lord your God. Obey the Lord your God and follow his commands and decrees that I give you today."

DEUTERONOMY 27:9

However, if you do not obey the Lord your God and do not carefully follow all his commands and decrees I am giving you today, all these curses will come upon you and overtake you.

DEUTERONOMY 28:15

The Lord will bring a nation against you from far away, from the ends of the earth, like an eagle swooping down, a nation whose language you will not understand.

DEUTERONOMY 28:49

For we are God's workmanship, created in Christ Jesus to do good works, which God prepared in advance for us to do.

EPHESIANS 2:10

And we know that in all things God works for the good of those who love him, who have been called according to his purpose.

ROMANS 8:28

Chapter 27

I have loved you with an everlasting love; I have drawn you with loving-kindness.

JEREMIAH 31:3

Brothers, we do not want you to be ignorant about those who fall asleep, or to grieve like the rest of men, who have no hope.

1 THESSALONIANS 4:13

APPENDIX 2

Praying Scripture

One of the most powerful ways you can pray is to pray God's Word right back to Him. Here are some Scripture prayers to help you develop this practice. These were used several years ago when our church was praying specifically for spiritual awakening. In 2004 God answered our prayers with more than five hundred decisions made for Christ during a week of meetings.

Father, we praise You because You are the Lord. We sing praises to You—all of us do! You rule over the nations, therefore we place our hope in You. Oh God of hope, fill us with all joy and peace as we trust in You so that we may overflow with hope by the power of Your Holy Spirit.

ROMANS 15:11–13

Oh God, You are faithful. Our confidence is not in ourselves; we are confident because You will keep us strong to the end. You will make us blameless on the day of our Lord Jesus Christ. You've called us into fellowship with Your Son, Jesus Christ our Lord, and You are faithful.

1 CORINTHIANS 1:8–9

Father, thank You that You demonstrated Your own love for us in this: while we were yet sinners, Christ died for us.

ROMANS 5:8

How great is the love the Father has lavished on us, that we should be called children of God!

1 JOHN 3:1

Father, let all that we do as Your people be demonstrations of the Spirit's power. Don't allow us to depend on wise and persuasive words or tactics but rather on the Spirit's power so that the faith we proclaim will not rest on men's wisdom but on God's power.

1 CORINTHIANS 2:4–5

What then shall we say in response to the world? If God is for us, who can be against us? You, Oh Lord, who did not spare Your own Son, but gave Him up for us all—how will You not also, along with Him, graciously give us all things?

ROMANS 8:31–32

Thank You, Lord, that we are more than conquerors through You who loves us. For I am convinced that neither death nor life, neither angels nor demons, neither the present nor the future, not any powers, neither height nor depth, nor anything else in all creation, will be able to separate us from the love of God that is in Christ Jesus our Lord.

ROMANS 8:37–39

And that is what we are! The reason the world doesn't know us is that it didn't know Him. Dear friends, now we are children of God, and what we will be has not yet been made known. But we know that when Jesus appears, we shall be like Him, for we shall see Him as He is. Thank You, Lord, that we are Your very own children.

1 JOHN 3:2

Lord, we ask that You pour Your very own love not only in us but also through us. Since You so loved the world, we also ought to love one another. No one has ever seen You, but if we love one another, You live in us, and Your love will be made complete in us

1 JOHN 4:11–12

Our neighbors, loved ones, and coworkers will know You because they will experience Your love. And this is my prayer: that your love may abound more and more in knowledge and depth of insight, so that you may be able to discern what is best and may be pure and blameless until the day of Christ, filled with the fruit of righteousness that comes through Jesus Christ—to the glory and praise of God.

PHILIPPIANS 1:9–11

Oh God, may I never boast except in the cross of our Lord Jesus Christ, through which the world has been crucified to me, and I to the world. This world has nothing that compares to the glory of knowing You. I will crucify any desire, any lust, anything in this world that attempts to lure me away from You. Thank You for the peace and mercy that dwell in me as I do this very thing.

GALATIANS 6:14–16

Faith is being sure of what we hope for and certain of what we do not see.

HEBREWS 11:1

And without faith it is impossible to please You, because anyone who comes to You must believe that You exist and that You reward those who earnestly seek You. Oh God, we believe!

HEBREWS 11:6

As we pray for awakening, Lord, we acknowledge the truth that though we live in the world, we do not wage war as the world does. The weapons we fight with are not the weapons of this world. On the contrary, they have divine power to demolish strongholds. We demolish arguments and every pretension that sets itself up against the knowledge of God, and we take captive every thought to make it obedient to Christ.

2 CORINTHIANS 10:3–5

Father, You are Lord—gracious, compassionate, slow to anger and rich in love.

PSALM 145:8

I wait for You. My soul waits, and in Your Word, I put my hope.

PSALM 130:5

Father, we have confidence before You that we can ask for anything! Because we obey Your commands and do what pleases You.

1 JOHN 3:21–22

Father, let us not be like those who are asleep, but let us be alert and self-controlled, putting on faith and love as a breastplate and the hope of salvation as a helmet. For You didn't appoint us to suffer wrath but to receive salvation through our Lord Jesus Christ.

1 THESSALONIANS 5:6–9

APPENDIX 3

Scripture for When You Doubt

When You Doubt God's Power

2 Chronicles 20:6
O Lord, God of our fathers, are you not the God who is in heaven? You rule over all the kingdoms of the nations. Power and might are in your hand, and no one can withstand you.

2 Chronicles 25:8
Even if you go and fight courageously in battle, God will overthrow you before the enemy, for God has the power to help or to overthrow.

Job 24:22
But God drags away the mighty by his power; though they become established, they have no assurance of life.

Job 30:18
In his great power [God] becomes like clothing to me; he binds me like the neck of my garment.

Psalm 66:3
Say to God, "How awesome are your deeds! So great is your power that your enemies cringe before you."

Job 36:22
God is exalted in his power. Who is a teacher like him?

Psalm 68:35
You are awesome, O God, in your sanctuary; the God of Israel gives power and strength to his people. Praise be to God!

Jeremiah 10:12

But God made the earth by his power; he founded the world by his wisdom and stretched out the heavens by his understanding.

Matthew 22:29

Jesus replied, "You are in error because you do not know the Scriptures or the power of God."

Acts 6:8

Now Stephen, a man full of God's grace and power, did great wonders and miraculous signs among the people.

Romans 1:16

I am not ashamed of the gospel, because it is the power of God for the salvation of everyone who believes: first for the Jew, then for the Gentile.

Romans 1:20

For since the creation of the world God's invisible qualities—his eternal power and divine nature—have been clearly seen, being understood from what has been made, so that men are without excuse.

Romans 9:22

What if God, choosing to show his wrath and make his power known, bore with great patience the objects of his wrath—prepared for destruction?

Romans 15:13

May the God of hope fill you with all joy and peace as you trust in him, so that you may overflow with hope by the power of the Holy Spirit.

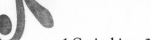

1 Corinthians 2:5

So that your faith might not rest on men's wisdom, but on God's power.

When You Doubt God's Concern

Deuteronomy 11:12

It is a land the Lord your God cares for; the eyes of the Lord your God are continually on it from the beginning of the year to its end.

Deuteronomy 30:3

Then the Lord your God will restore your fortunes and have compassion on you and gather you again from all the nations where he scattered you.

2 Chronicles 30:9

If you return to the Lord, then your brothers and your children will be shown compassion by their captors and will come back to this land, for the Lord your God is gracious and compassionate. He will not turn his face from you if you return to him.

Isaiah 30:18

Yet the Lord longs to be gracious to you; he rises to show you compassion. For the Lord is a God of justice. Blessed are all who wait for him!

Jonah 3:10

When God saw what they did and how they turned from their evil ways, he had compassion and did not bring upon them the destruction he had threatened.

Psalm 116:5

The Lord is gracious and righteous; our God is full of compassion.

Zechariah 10:6

I will strengthen the house of Judah and save the house of Joseph. I will restore them because I have compassion on them. They will be as though I had not rejected them, for I am the Lord their God and I will answer them.

2 Corinthians 1:3

Praise be to the God and Father of our Lord Jesus Christ, the Father of compassion and the God of all comfort.

Exodus 34:6

And he passed in front of Moses, proclaiming, "The Lord, the Lord, the compassionate and gracious God, slow to anger, abounding in love and faithfulness."

Deuteronomy 7:9

Know therefore that the Lord your God is God; he is the faithful God, keeping his covenant of love to a thousand generations of those who love him and keep his commands.

Deuteronomy 7:12

If you pay attention to these laws and are careful to follow them, then the Lord your God will keep his covenant of love with you, as he swore to your forefathers.

When You Doubt God's Wisdom

Job 12:13
To God belong wisdom and power; counsel and understanding are his.

Ecclesiastes 2:26
To the man who pleases him, God gives wisdom, knowledge and happiness, but to the sinner he gives the task of gathering and storing up wealth to hand it over to the one who pleases God. This too is meaningless, a chasing after the wind.

Luke 2:52
And Jesus grew in wisdom and stature, and in favor with God and men.

Romans 11:33
Oh, the depth of the riches of the wisdom and knowledge of God! How unsearchable his judgments, and his paths beyond tracing out!

1 Corinthians 1:30
It is because of him that you are in Christ Jesus, who has become for us wisdom from God—that is, our righteousness, holiness and redemption.

1 Corinthians 2:7
No, we speak of God's secret wisdom, a wisdom that has been hidden and that God destined for our glory before time began.

Ephesians 1:17
I keep asking that the God of our Lord Jesus Christ, the glorious Father, may give you the Spirit of wisdom and revelation, so that you may know him better.

Colossians 1:9

For this reason, since the day we heard about you, we have not stopped praying for you and asking God to fill you with the knowledge of his will through all spiritual wisdom and understanding.

James 1:5

If any of you lacks wisdom, he should ask God, who gives generously to all without finding fault, and it will be given to him.

Revelation 7:12

Saying: "Amen! Praise and glory and wisdom and thanks and honor and power and strength be to our God for ever and ever. Amen!"

When You Doubt God's Plan

Psalm 57:2

I cry out to God Most High, to God, who fulfills [his purpose] for me.

Romans 8:28

And we know that in all things God works for the good of those who love him, who have been called according to his purpose.

2 Corinthians 5:5

Now it is God who has made us for this very purpose and has given us the Spirit as a deposit, guaranteeing what is to come.

Philippians 2:13

For it is God who works in you to will and to act according to his good purpose.

Hebrews 6:17

Because God wanted to make the unchanging nature of his purpose very clear to the heirs of what was promised, he confirmed it with an oath.

Revelation 17:17

For God has put it into their hearts to accomplish his purpose by agreeing to give the beast their power to rule, until God's words are fulfilled.

Jeremiah 29:11

"For I know the plans I have for you," declares the Lord, "plans to prosper you and not to harm you, plans to give you hope and a future."

Psalm 33:11

But the plans of the Lord stand firm forever, the purposes of his heart through all generations.

Proverbs 19:21

Many are the plans in a man's heart, but it is the Lord's purpose that prevails.

Proverbs 3:5-6

Trust in the Lord with all your heart and lean not on your own understanding; in all your ways acknowledge him, and he will make your paths straight.

When You Doubt God's Love

1 Kings 8:23
O Lord, God of Israel, there is no God like you in heaven above or on earth below—you who keep your covenant of love with your servants who continue wholeheartedly in your way.

1 Kings 10:9
Praise be to the Lord your God, who has delighted in you and placed you on the throne of Israel. Because of the Lord's eternal love for Israel, he has made you king, to maintain justice and righteousness.

Nehemiah 9:17
They refused to listen and failed to remember the miracles you performed among them. They became stiff-necked and in their rebellion appointed a leader in order to return to their slavery. But you are a forgiving God, gracious and compassionate, slow to anger and abounding in love. Therefore you did not desert them.

Psalm 42:8
By day the Lord directs his love, at night his song is with me—a prayer to the God of my life.

Psalm 52:8
But I am like an olive tree flourishing in the house of God; I trust in God's unfailing love for ever and ever.

Psalm 57:3
He sends from heaven and saves me, rebuking those who hotly pursue me; "Selah" God sends his love and his faithfulness.

Psalm 136:2
Give thanks to the God of gods. "His love endures forever."

Joel 2:13

Rend your heart and not your garments. Return to the Lord your God, for he is gracious and compassionate, slow to anger and abounding in love, and he relents from sending calamity.

Zephaniah 3:17

The Lord your God is with you, he is mighty to save. He will take great delight in you, he will quiet you with his love, he will rejoice over you with singing.

Romans 5:5

And hope does not disappoint us, because God has poured out his love into our hearts by the Holy Spirit, whom he has given us.

Romans 5:8

But God demonstrates his own love for us in this: While we were still sinners, Christ died for us.

Romans 8:39

Neither height nor depth, nor anything else in all creation, will be able to separate us from the love of God that is in Christ Jesus our Lord.

2 Corinthians 13:11

Finally, brothers, good-by. Aim for perfection, listen to my appeal, be of one mind, live in peace. And the God of love and peace will be with you.

Ephesians 5:2

And live a life of love, just as Christ loved us and gave himself up for us as a fragrant offering and sacrifice to God.

For God so loved the world
that he gave his one and only Son,
that whoever believes in him
shall not perish but have eternal life.

—

JOHN 3:16

Endnotes

1 Denver Cheddie, *How Does God Speak to Us Today?*, http://www.bibleissues.org/voice1.html.

2 Exodus 33 gives an account of Moses' prayer life and says this about conversations between God and Moses: "The Lord would speak to Moses face to face, as a man speaks with his friend" (v. 11).

3 I'm not going to take time to share my vision, but you can read what God communicated to me through it by reading Galatians 4:1–9.

4 Ziya Meral, "Bearing the Silence of God," http://www.christianitytoday.com/ct/2008/march/29.41.html?start=2.

5 Hannah Hurnard, *Hinds' Feet on High Places* (Wheaton, IL: Living Books, a division of Tyndale House Publishers, 1975), 156–57.

6 David C. Pack, *The Keys to Dynamic Prayer*, http://rcg.org/articles/tktdp.html.

7 http://www.thefreedictionary.com/wisdom.

8 Caleb Woodbridge, *Quotes from "The Problem of Pain" by C. S. Lewis*, http://blog.calebwoodbridge.com/2009/04/quotes-from-problem-of-pain-by-c-s.html.

9 C. S. Lewis, *The Lion, the Witch and the Wardrobe*, http://outofborderland.blogspot.com.

My Notes from This Study

My Notes from This Study

My Notes from This Study

My Notes from This Study

My Notes from This Study

Leighann McCoy

is the prayer and women's minister at Thompson Station Church in Thompson Station, TN, where her husband Tom is the senior pastor.

Her books include *Spiritual Warfare for Women, Women Overcoming Fear,* and *Meet Me at the Manger and I'll Lead You to the Cross.* Leighann lives in Franklin, TN, and is the mother of two daughters, one son, and a son-in-law: Mikel (Austin), Kaleigh, and T.J. Her favorite role is that of Nana to her granddaughter, Misty.